THE VIOLENT IMAGINATION

The Violent Imagination

Robin Fox

 RUTGERS UNIVERSITY PRESS
New Brunswick and London

Acknowledgment is given for use of the following previously published material:

"The Conference of Foules," *The Cambridge Review* 103, no. 2270 (1982):293–295.
"Image de la Comtesse," *Bulletin de la Société des Professeurs Français en Amérique* (1978–79):68–69.
"What the Hunter Saw," in *Reflections: The Anthropological Muse*, ed. J. Iain Prattis (Washington D.C.: American Anthropological Association, 1985), pp. 70–73.

Library of Congress Cataloging-in-Publication Data
Fox, Robin, 1934–
  The violent imagination / Robin Fox.
    p. cm.
  ISBN 0-8135-1367-7
  I. Title.
PS3556.0948V86 1989   88-21759
811'.54—dc19   CIP

British Cataloging-in-Publication information available

for Lin

Contents

FOUR: TOWARD A MORE PERFECT DISSOLUTION

ACKNOWLEDGMENTS

Several people were instrumental in encouraging me to persevere. Early on, Paul Friedrich, Howard Moss, and Nathaniel Tarn made valuable suggestions about the verse; but I have not felt able to take up wholeheartedly Tarn's invitation to "join the twentieth century." Along the way, Karyl Roosevelt, Henry Hardy, and Sean Magee were particularly encouraging. But above all I want to thank my daughters. Kate sustained me with her belief in the book and her insistence that I continue, to say nothing of her practical help. Ellie patiently typed a constantly changing manuscript, and Anne's quizzical skepticism helped keep me honest. Together they prevented me from ever getting too serious with myself. Suzanne Grossman, actress, screenwriter, and brilliant translator of Feydeau, is duly acknowledged in the proper place. Kenneth Arnold and the staff of the Rutgers University Press made a difficult production job unfailingly pleasant. Becky Staples was much more than a copyeditor— she was one of my best critics. The dedication is to my wife for her loving optimism, which makes me doubt my most cynical conclusions. We can only hope that she is right and I am wrong, and take heart that this is usually so.

R. F.
Princeton, New Jersey
July 1988

INTRODUCTION

. . . .

Yes, Virginia, this is yet another 'commentary on the human condition.' Despite the ponderous overtones, this is really a serious tradition and one I am glad to belong to. But the conditions under which we now have to write such commentaries have drastically changed. Two things have altered our sense of ourselves radically: the daily prospect of total annihilation for our species and our very recent awareness of our ancientness as a species (with all the implications this has for an understanding of ourselves).

It is a sad irony that this latter crucial knowledge, which promises to transform our ideas of what we are and what we can hope for in the future, has been acquired at almost exactly the time when we are threatening to make that future impossible. We are like someone who has been handed a great fortune along with instructions to commit suicide.

1

Reason, imagination, and violence today coexist in a way we can only try to analyze or express; we can't seem to do much about them. But the two cultures of Reason and Imagination—the wrong basis for the antagonism between the humanities and the sciences—do not exist out there in the world; they only exist in our cognitive reconstruction of it. Before Plato they were not sundered, but before Plato there was not much science either. Yet Plato wanted the Poets and Artists out of The Republic because, as Eric Havelock rightly observes, they laid claim to a rival method for arriving at the truth, not just a superior capacity for entertainment. So Plato argues for their banishment.

This perhaps necessary divorce, however, like so much of the Platonic heritage, may yet cost us dearly. It may yet cost us everything. As Voltaire, in 1770, passionately declaimed:

"O Platon tant admiré, j'ai peur que vous ne vous ayez conté que des fables, et que vous n'ayez jamais parlé qu'en sophismes. O Platon! vous avez fait bien plus de mal que vous ne croyez. Comment cela? me demendera-t-on: je ne le dirai pas." (Dictionnaire Philosophique) Why wouldn't he say what the damage was? Perhaps because at that time it had not been fully assessed. Perhaps because Voltaire sensed the dangerous fragmentation that Plato had wrought, but had not seen its full effects. If that is the case, then Voltaire was truly prophetic. And again there is a real irony, because when Plato wanted to express the great truth of truths, in the *Timaeus,* he resorted to the language of myth and poetry, and obviously meant us to take him seriously. (Which leads me to wonder if the mass of the Socratic dialogues are not perhaps some kind of send up: a vast satire on the misuse of reason.)

But the reintegration that our condition cries out for cannot be on a pre-Platonic basis: a tribal, heroic, oral basis. Our capacity for literate communication and self annihilation has outrun that possibility. Yet we do not seem able to make the imaginative/rational leap into the state of consciousness needed to handle this monstrous situation that we have ourselves created out of the Platonic sundering of reason and imagination. Where must we start in trying to re-understand ourselves?

The foregoing is set off because it is the beginning of an academic, argumentative piece of writing still in progress; but it serves just as well as the opening blast of this book. Indeed, when this project first thought itself through me, such pieces were included in it. There was this one, ponderously titled "Consciousness Out of Context: History, Progress, Evolution, and the Post-post-industrial Society." (Well, that's the way we do things in our little world: first stun 'em with a title, then wow 'em with an argument.) Another piece, already published, would have been "The Violent Imagination" (P. Marsh and A. Campbell, eds., *Violence and*

Aggression [Oxford: Blackwell, 1982]). But, as you see, I have simply appropriated the title of that one. The third heavy would have been "On Inhuman Nature and Unnatural Rights" (*Encounter* 58, no. 4 [1982]). Its original title was "Rational Ethics and Human Nature," but Mel Lasky, the wise and cunning editor of that remarkable magazine, thought up the new one as both smarter and more to the point. The point? The point of all these pieces is that we are indeed living in a state of "consciousness out of context"; that the true context of our consciousness was the upper-paleolithic (our "environment of evolutionary adaptedness" as the jargon has it); that in this environment there was a harmony of our evolved attributes as a species, including our intelligence, our imagination, our violence, (and hence our violent imagination), our reason and our passions—a harmony that has been lost; that this harmony did not mean peace, love, and justice for all, but rather simply that the pieces fit together in a way that served to further the interests of the species directly, and above all not to threaten its existence as a species.

This is no longer true. Partly it is simply a matter of scale and complexity, but with these goes fragmentation. Eliot and Henry Adams among others deplored the fragmentation as much as I do, but from a very different perspective and a different sense of our species' history. Eliot could take us as far back as the sensibilities of the Metaphysical poets (late seventeenth century) for his time of harmony; Adams could go back to the eleventh century and Mont St. Michel and Chartres. But in the evolutionary perspective these were sadly fragmented times in which reason, imagination, violence, and curiosity were all working against each other, and passion was deeply suspect unless it was religious passion, and even then (and perhaps even more.) The basics remained the same: zealotry, xenophobia, greed, lust, gullibility of the many, and power hunger of the few; the evil dominance of the idea by which we live and for which we will die and which is wrong; the search for meaning that is our original sin and that either elevates us to godhead or reduces us to foaming fanatics when our answer is threatened. All these were surely there from the start of our humanity. But what we find hard to imagine is that they could work together and harmonize and produce, for the species, a positive result.

This does not seem possible to our modern fragmented consciousness, where every frenetic addition to our already overburdened civilization seems to produce a serendipitous disaster. "Modern" in this view means after ten thousand years before the present (BP) for most societies; and today even those that retained the harmony are not untouched by the easy if short-lived triumph of the fragmented civilizations, whose "specialization" brings short-term benefits and long-term destruction.

So that's what is in the heavy articles that were originally to have appeared in this book; at least those are the conclusions. I wanted to include them as part of my plea to reverse the fragmentation. But the tyranny of the idea is implacable. (See "Design Failure," in Part Four). Such a product was impossible: it was a denial of established and sacred categories; it was more than error, it was witchcraft. (The social anthropologists have analyzed this very well—the fact that the unclean, polluted, and dangerous is that which offends the established system of categories.) So I took them out, and the result is different, but still makes its point especially if taken with the heavies as a chaser. Here, rather than rubbing the readers' noses in "the message," I have sketched it, hinted at it, approached it obliquely through themes and variations, made it implicit in the very structure and content of what follows, and even introduced a fashionable air of "metalogue," insofar as the total structure of the effort (including the real presence of the absent articles) makes its own point about the sources and dangers of, and maybe even solutions to, the fragmentation. But I really don't have any solutions, only hints and guesses: perhaps only the cries and whimpers of an animal trapped in the awful consequences of its own success—a situation to which it will not admit because it is too terrifying to face. We have met The Enemy, as Pogo declared, and He is Us. All our efforts to improve the deteriorating situation seem to backfire.

One of these backfiring efforts appears to be the academic/scientific mode itself. One fears to abandon it much as true believers fear to abandon their religions, but one fears equally to get stuck in it and thus perpetuate the already unsatisfactory situation. So here I try another way: a kind of "theme and variations" approach. Such academic-style argument as tries to rear its head is quickly turned into a parody of itself. The themes are approached from a variety of angles, and through different modes of expression, and are differently mixed and mingled; every which way, one hopes, but boring. And the "metalogical" scheme, which has started with a plea to reject Plato's banishment of the artists from the Republic of Science and Virtue, then tries to illustrate some of the consequences of letting them back in. ("Putting the poetry back into politics," as E. P. Thompson has recently argued and demonstrated.) Indeed, if the whole thing could be set to music and staged it would perhaps make this point more effectively. It is hard to make the right impact with a purely linear medium like a "book."

4

And this is not a plea for entertainment—although that would follow—but for a new kind of consciousness that will transcend the fragmentation of our times (if you'll forgive the pomposity.) I don't know yet what that will be, so I can only plead for an exploration of it, and for us to face up to not only the dangers, but the virtues, of the violent imagination, as opposed to those of reason, intelligence, culture, or especially "artificial intelligence." I veer between mild optimism and total pessimism; but the pessimism may alarm and alert and so serve a useful purpose. The implicit cynicism (of course the last, battered refuge of an idealist) is more troubling; but again, the fear of being driven to it is perhaps a healthy fear.

I have resisted demands to supply "linking material"; the whole point here is to keep the readers off guard so they have constantly to be making the links themselves: between the dilemmas of the battery hens and those of the moral relativists; between the condition of Sweden and the fallacy of historical progress; between the author's implicit plea for a total society and his totally contradictory defense of individualism when faced with the inquisitorial consequences of one (despite his cynicism over the insects); between the estimation of the imaginative (cultural) transformation of power by authority, and the role of violence in ritual and sexual passion; between the art of the paleolithic, the symbolism of the bullfight, the basic human design failure, and the psalm's "tumor" and despair at wasted consciousness and meaningless death; between the nightmare of history from which we all, like Stephen Daedalus, are trying to awake, and the author's nightmare about history, which is itself part of Vishnu's world dream—the maya in which we are entrapped, or, if the intrusive philosopher of mind is correct, in which we entrap ourselves, and of which Vishnu (Christ/God) is himself a product; between the rationalizations of violence by the highly rational purveyors of a national revolution, and the fantasy salvation-by-sexual-violence of two latter-day products of that enterprise; between a provincial Colombian bullfight with its search for meaningful death as a response to an existence without meaning, and the contrivance of a bizarre death-through-sex by a contemporary New Yorker, itself linked to the paleolithic cult of the bear sacrifice; between the vision of the hunter before his xenophobic murder, and that of George Washington before his terrifying sentence; always between the highly general and argumentative (and usually blank verse) ruminations, and the lyrics (some of which are indeed words for songs) that pull the questions down to the most painful and comic intimacies of personal lives while constantly questioning the doubtful possibility of salvation through eros—the Romantic solution; and sometimes a mixture of elements that looks for the general in the particular, and vice versa. But I've already preempted too much of what I have declared to be the reader's privilege. The sheer complexity of the possibilities, once grasped, should convey to the reader why logical academic argument with its own linear limitations cannot sustain the themes, and why they so easily tip over into poetry and myth. Perhaps this itself is the clue to the harmony of the lost past and the possibilities of the almost lost future.

In any case, my hermeneutic colleagues tell me, the text, now written and out there in the world, isn't mine any more. So go to it. The links I make may not be yours at all. Stephen Spender told me that Eliot told him that what was uppermost in his mind during the writing of *The Waste Land* was Wagner's *Ring*. Despite the wailing of the Rhine Maidens, I would never have guessed this. The whole poem looks different to me now, but this does not invalidate the "linking themes" that we had seen in it before this revelation of the poet's preoccupation.

Some readers, while grasping the point of Part Two, have nevertheless asked why I particularly chose George Washington, and why the American Revolution, rather than the Russian, French, or English. (How easily people forget that there was an English revolution.) As it happens, my first choice was the English fracas, and an original sketch has this as the trial of Oliver Cromwell. But as Part Three shows, I have spent most of my adult life trying to come to terms with the puzzling consequences of the Anglo-American civil war. As the bicentennial came and went, I was driven more and more to thinking about the Revolt of the Rationalists, and the Utopian hopes that were its consequence. What appears here is really an extract with adaptations from an epic intended for the bicentennial. While well regarded—as they say—it was never produced, if only because agonizing reappraisal had gone out of fashion and no one wanted a play in which George Washington gets hung, drawn, and quartered. Understandably, it lost out to the super patriotic if dreadfully dull *Valley Forge* in the Hallmark Hall of Fame Television Theater Stakes. The attempted television version was written in collaboration with Suzanne Grossman, since I had no idea how to adapt for television. While what I use here is dialogue that I wrote myself (except for a few words of Washington's final address to the court), Suzanne did a lot of the research with me and her notion of the whole undoubtedly had an influence on shaping the parts, so her indispensable collaboration is gratefully acknowledged.

This book is very much work in progress. It has to be seen as part of the larger scheme. Nothing is settled here; it is mostly hinted at. But nothing is particularly obscure either except the odd literary joke. We pedants are incorrigible jokesters with a particular fondness for bad puns. It is what separates us from mere intellectuals. (You will already have noticed the title's deliberate play on that of Lionel Trilling's most famous book, to say nothing of one by C. Wright Mills. Of course, the counterpoint is deliberate; the scepticism over the liberal version of optimism is real. But closer reading will show that, oddly enough, Trilling and I are not too far apart: see especially his *Beyond Culture*.) And while the "message" (God help us!) is serious enough, it is also playful. So let us remember Huizinga: "The play-concept as such is of a higher order than seriousness. For seriousness seeks to exclude play, whereas play can well include seriousness." Or hear the 2,000-year-old Mel Brooks: "The greatest comedy plays against the greatest tragedy. Comedy is a red-rubber ball and if you throw it against a soft, funny wall, it will not come back. But if you throw it against the hard wall of ultimate reality it will bounce back and be very lively." In the end, perhaps, we must laugh one another, or die.

In token whereof I give you the following as an appetizer:

RESEARCH REPORT: CONVERSATION
AFTER A SABBATICAL

"So you've written a new book?"
"Yes"
"Tell us then
the number of the pages   publication
date and price   the publisher   and yes
the subject matter   theme   that sort of thing"

"The subject matter is intact   The book—
well   it was written in a different way
I wrote in sometimes with my fingers dry

7

and sometimes wet with wine or honey on
an undulating   brown   and scented body

I wrote a lot—a thousand words a day
for—well—a hundred days   A lot of words
At each day's end we would make love   and I
would lick them off   or scented sweat would smudge
the wine-dark prose   But every day the parchment
would be there fresh and clear   and I would write"

"But   then   you have . . ."
                              "No book?   But don't you see
I still have her body there to read
and when I'm finished reading   then to write
It is my book   And now I must go work
Work   Work   Work   I'm such a puritan"

ne

Diary

Of a

Superfluous

Race

THREE BASIC LYRICS
(to establish some basic things)

> *It is because of the difficulty of translating right-*
> *hemispherical processes into the logical, verbal*
> *formulations of the left brain that some emissions*
> *into ego consciousness of archetypal images are*
> *perceived as numinous, awesome, and mysterious,*
> *or uncanny, preternaturally strange. They seem to*
> *be clad in primordial authority undetermined by*
> *anything known or learned.*
>
> Victor Turner, *Body, Brain, and Culture*

. . . .

CAROUSEL
(Asbury Park, Summer)

I smile indulgently to see
the carousel go spinning by—
the children calling out to me
to get aboard   at least to try

I shake my head   demur   decline
I'm too old for the roundabout
Those screaming joys are yours not mine
I'll look on while you wave and shout

But then I am afraid to look
afraid because I know I'll see
the phantom from the story book
the ghostly child who looks like me

11

Staring from his painted horse
he smiles his never changing smile
and whirls precisely on his course
mile after jangling   dizzy mile

He nods with every rise and fall
he beckons me at every turn
he never speaks   but seems to call
his eyes are cold   but seem to burn

When to the phantom spinning by
I whisper   (not to seem absurd)
"Are you the phantom or am I?"
he spins and smiles without a word

It stops   he goes   the children call
"Daddy you look so unwell"
"It makes me dizzy   that is all—
just looking at the carousel"

THE FOOL SINGS OF HIS SKULL AND ITS CONTENTS

Nun sag'! Nichts weißt du, was ich dich frage:
jetzt meld', was du weißt;
denn etwas mußt du doch wissen.

Wagner, *Parsifal*

Oh the queer things that go on
under this bony cap
they make me want to sing
and dance and curse and clap
they make me want to laugh
and cry and storm and shout—
but most of all they make me want
to shake the thing about

Oh the odd things that go on
inside this bony bowl

they call 'em mind and thought
they call 'em spirit and soul
they call 'em moods and states
and other fancy names—
but nobody ever found the rules
for their funny little games

Oh the strange things that go on
and on and on and on
things that are always there
things that have come and gone
things that confuse the day
things that disturb the night—
all those puzzles and problems
and nobody gets 'em right

But of all the things that go on—
that leak in through the ears
that jump in through the eyes—
the things I mostly fears
are the things that were always there
What they are you never know
but they've got you trapped in the bony cage
and though you argue   plead and rage—
they'll never let you go

HE APOLOGIZES TO HER FOR COMPARING HER EYES TO THE WINGS OF CAPTIVE HUMMINGBIRDS USED IN NAVAHO RITUALS

Forget the hummingbirds   I didn't mean
to make you pretty speeches   but your eyes
demanded metaphors   and I have seen
the captive bird and all that it implies

That's no excuse for rhetoric   I know—
but form imprisons function like a child
enmeshed in discipline   It should be so
else childish function   wordlike   would run wild

13

The bird   when free   is but another bird—
a formless phrase   a brief emotion spent
a frozen movement   fluttering unheard—
captive   it's a magic argument

So I have no excuse my love but this—
a need to capture   in my cage of words
a meaning deeper than a formless kiss
on eyelids brushing me like frightened birds

Forgive me my formality   my speech—
my futile effort at control—unwise
because it will not last   We cannot each
escape the consequences of our eyes

THE PARADOX OF CONSCIOUSNESS (O Muse
I sing) as such is not confined to man
If we define it as a minimum
"Matter aware of its own existence" then
we cannot be sure that animals do not
possess a rudimentary form of it

Full consciousness is a unique event
in earthly history   We can be sure
our solar system lacks it   but about
the universe we cannot be so certain
If there is organic life there is
the possibility of consciousness
The very number of the galaxies
makes the existence of it probable

THE CONFERENCE OF FOULES

La turba che rimase li, selvaggia
parea del loco, rimrando intorno
come colui che nove cose assaggia

Dante, *Divina Commedia: Purgatorio*, Canto I.52

. . . .

The Cities of the Battery Hens were in trouble, and the Guardians, knowing that the trouble was endogenous, had cunningly assembled what they thought to be the cleverest and wisest of the hens in the same place to see if they could come up with their own solutions. The hens had no idea there were Guardians at all (they never saw them) and were under the impression that they were responsible for their own lives. Some rather daring intellects among them had suggested that 'the forces of history' or 'the species struggle' or something such was responsible—but the pragmatists paid them little heed.

So they sat there, one hen to a tiny cage, immobile, beaks plucked out, their legs bred away, their feathers reduced, their bodies flooded with hormones and chemicals, clucking and producing, clucking and laying, laying, laying. A conveyor belt took away the eggs, they knew not where or why. But the eggs were tasteless, the hens listless. They died easily from contagious diseases that racked the cities despite the massive sanitary precautions of the Guardians. Mostly they sickened from mysterious maladies that no one could diagnose; they simply gave up laying, gave up clucking, became glassy-eyed, and eventually died.

The wise ones, however, clucking and swallowing their uniform, vitamin-rich, hormone-treated food pellets, were busy analyzing the situation.

The first to speak was the wise old economist. She was very insistent. "Facts, facts, facts," she said, "and then models, models, models." She continued—to a chorus of approving clucks—"We need the finest input-output model of the Battery World Economy (BWE); we need to feed it with the richest information from every possible source; we must analyze the flow of pellets, the state of sanitation, the infrastructure of the cages, the gross world product (GWP) of eggs, the huge differential between the advanced battery economies (ABE) and the underdeveloped barnyard economies (UBE), the problems of barnyard to battery transition, and why huge transfers of cages to the barnyard won't work." There was tumultuous applause. "Give that hen a prize," they said, and they did give her a prize. "How decidedly post-Kenyesian," they said, and felt a lot had been achieved. They adjourned to sip at their sugar water (also laced with hormones, of course, and vitamins, of course), then resumed.

The political scientist hen was not so sure. "It is not clear," she said sagely, "that the question is fundamentally economic. The question is one of power: who controls the economy? Our problem is that we do not know. There are many assumptions, some of which can be dismissed as purely supernatural, like the theory of the Guardians" (much clucking and chuckling and even outright laughter), "but the question remains— who controls the pellets?" (much muttering and head wagging). "If only this question could be settled," she said, "perhaps we could regulate our own lives better and cure the terrible malaise. It will, of course, require massive research, since the source of power over the pellets is obviously multifactoral, multifunctional, and multidimensional."

There was much agreement—if not much enthusiasm. The hens were uneasy at the thought that they were not the masters of their fate. They accepted it intellectually—after all, they were intellectuals, and if things were indeed entirely as they seemed to be, then there would be no mysteries to solve, and they would have no excuse for being. But "mysterious" problems of "power" bothered them.

It was with great relief, therefore, that they turned to the famous architect, praised for the "near mystical" beauty of her vision and her compassion for the beings who inhabited her structures. "The problem seems to me," she said, "to be one of vision—literally." They were intrigued. "We are so restricted in our ability to *see* each other because of the structure of the cages." The excitement was palpable. "If we cannot see each other properly, how can we effectively communicate?" True, true, they clucked, how indeed? "My solution, my architectural solution, is to redesign the cages with rods of mirror glass. Bank upon bank of reflecting cages with slender mirror-glass rods, stacked in quadrangles rather than aisles. We could not only communicate more readily, but live within a vision of shining—but utilitarian—beauty."

The applause was deafening. The clucking uncontrollable. "Mystical," they said; "visionary," they said; "astounding genius—give that hen a medal." And they did give her a medal. When the noise died down, the psychiatric hen (socially oriented) could only come as an anticlimax, but she did her best.

"Our problem lies at the psychosomatic interface," she said (groans, yawns—insofar as beakless mouths can yawn). "Basically, the hens lack a sense of *personal well-being*. This leads to stress and breakdown. Re-designing the cages is all very well, but without massive research into the *attitudes* and *motivations* of our fellow egg-producing persons, we shall never understand our malaise. The essential problem is one of *adequate adjustment.* Given the perfect environment, why do the organisms not adjust perfectly? They are free from want, free from disease, free from fear of predators, free from all needs—but they are *not well adjusted.* We need massive research—multifactoral, multifunctional, and multidimensional—to discover how we can manipulate the cage environment and how we can *remotivate* the inhabitants to achieve well-being and health."

"Yes," interjected the political scientist, "but that doesn't solve the problem of who controls the pellets—you merely divert us from the real problem."

"Nonsense," said the great economist, "the real problem is with the productive infrastructure."

"Now, now," said the great architect, "all we need is vision and compassion."

"What price vision without power!" shouted the political scientist—and things looked like they were getting out of hand. The philosopher saved the day by turning the discussion to the semantics of the question, and everyone became totally engrossed in the business of the difference between "power *to* control" and "power *for* control"—except the political scientist. Everyone suspected her of prejudiced political leanings anyway. The sociologist then spoke, but no one understood her. It had something to do with the inevitability of the whole world of hendom converting to batteryism because of changed social consciousness consequent upon the social revolution in the imperialist battery cities, which itself was an epiphenomenon of the interaction between the rise of battery technology and the ideology of Persistent Egg Production (PEP) transformed into an imperialistic world battery economy in which . . . Everyone was clucking away to her neighbour by now and someone called for a sugar-water break, which, to everyone's relief, was agreed on.

Except by the Still Small Voice that had not spoken, interjected or even clucked during the above. "But you don't understand," it now interposed desperately. "We're asking the wrong questions."

Everyone looked amazed. Weren't they the best brains in the battery? How could they be asking the wrong questions? "Enlighten us, SSV," they said, sarcastically, while paying more attention to their sugar-water.

The Still Small Voice cocked her head as far sideways as the restrictions of the cage allowed. "Out there," she indicated, "is the barnyard whence, very recently, we came. Most chickens in the world live like that, and most have for most of their known existence." There were rumbles of obvious distaste at this indelicate topic, but the SSV persisted. "They live in the open except for roughly constructed roosts. They live in polygamous families, and the cock fertilizes their eggs. They have little nests of straw where they incubate their eggs and raise fluffy chicks who follow them about and peck and peep. They don't lay nearly as many eggs as we do, and the eggs are small and brown, but the chicks grow legs and feathers and peck at the ground for their food (more murmurs of distaste). It's true," said the SSV plaintively, "that they don't have our advantages—totally controlled environments with sanitation, food pellets with vitamins, scientifically designed cages, and high egg production. It's true the cocks fight among themselves and the hens are submissive to the cocks and have their own pecking order (clucks of horror), and it's true they peck in the dirt with real beaks for their food (more horror), but they don't die glassy-eyed, from unknown causes, and they see the sun and feel the wind and they survive. And that's what we did for most of our chicken history. Perhaps something went wrong?"

The chorus of abuse, sarcasm, and scorn that followed drowned out the odd cluck of agreement here and there.

The sociologist said that she would never have imagined that Narodniks were still flourishing, much less daring to express opinions. Everyone knew that the transition to batteryism was inevitable and this was just romantic populism.

The great economist complained that this kind of consideration could not be put into her input-output model—and how did knowing about the barnyard help improve the cages?

Or, for that matter, said the political scientist, solve the problem of who had power over the pellets and how to get it.

There was really no future, said the socially oriented psychiatrist, in a back-to-the-barnyard philosophy. The problem was with adjustment to the cages. The economist and the sociologist chorused together that all the barnyard hens were rushing to get into the battery cities anyway, and this trend was irreversible. So the issue could only be how to improve the cages and get more pellets. ("Power over the pellets," corrected the political scientist, but she was beginning to be ignored.)

The great architect was more constructive, more visionary, more compassionate. It was perfectly true, she said, that the barnyard-to-battery transition was inevitable, but the SSV had a point. The truly visionary and compassionate way to deal with this was to build cages that were aesthetically in tune with the indigenous barnyard culture—not to force our steel and concrete (or even glass) notions onto them (laughter) but to design cages from their own materials and in their own traditions. She proposed, therefore, that the cages be made of firm rods of twisted straw—the natural material of the barnyard—but of course beautifully braided, and the floors of the cages could be made of compacted dirt with a suitable polyurethane covering. The de-beaked, de-feathered, and de-legged hens would then feel less alienated from their traditional settings. We should not, she repeated, force our notions of the perfect cage upon them. Let the cage arise out of their own traditions and their 'well-being' would be more certain.

The applause was again tumultuous. "Constructive," they said; "compassionate," they said; "give that hen another medal." Of course, the diehards quibbled. "Infrastructure, infrastructure," said the economist. "No barnyards exist without massive subsidies." "Power—who builds the cages, is there a wings deal?" said the political scientist. "Romantic piffle," said the sociologist—but she was cut short by the general applause.

The Still Small Voice, however, was quite agitated by now. She became a Still Large Voice and heckled the multitude. "You still don't understand. Sure, the barnyard wasn't paradise—it isn't clear we should have been living in barnyards either, but we did, and we survived, and somehow it worked, and we still had our beaks and legs." ("Reactionary," they said, "romantic piffle.") The SSV (or SLV) continued above the hubbub: "But I'm not saying the barnyard was *the* answer—I'm saying it was about the best we could do. We're here to discuss why all the hens in the cages are falling over dead, damn it. Perhaps we shouldn't be in cages, or barnyards."

There was a shocked silence, broken when, with something between sadness and sarcasm, a querant demanded, "But how would they get the pellets to us?"

"Who," asked the political scientist, "are *they?*" But the Still Small Voice was insistent. "The battery cities, with all their technological wonders, are a few decades old; even the barnyards are only a few thousand years old. We were meant for neither. For millions of years our ancestors (groans) lived in the jungles. They only laid one or at most two clutches of eggs a year. But they kept their chicks around, and the chicks imprinted on their mothers and stayed in little families. They roamed the jungle for food in small territories, and groups of mothers were guarded by great cocks with brilliant combs and plumage that was always luxuriant with the greens of the forest and the oranges, reds, and purples of their arrogant displays. And they had great beaks, talons, and flashing spurs on their ankles, and they fought for territories and females and crowed defiance to their rivals at dawn. The rain rained on them and they snuggled in their nests; the sun warmed them and they strutted and pecked in the open places. They were killed by snakes and birds of prey; their eggs were eaten by reptiles and primitive mammals, but they hung on and flourished. There never was such fierce beauty in any ground birds as in their cocks, or such broody sexiness as in their hens. And they made eggs to make more chickens—not for its own sake as we do (or for whatever purposes the conveyor belt has for them—we don't know). They lived for themselves without the help of scientists and scholars and technicians. And this, my poor companions, was for millions and millions of years. This is what we are. What have we done to ourselves? That is what we should be asking, not how to get more artificial pellets and how to design better cages."

The sheer length of the speech had stilled them to silence. The sociologist broke it. "Brilliant," she said, "but I have only one question." "What is that?" asked the philosopher (who was happier with questions than with answers). "How do we get more pellets and how do we design better cages?"

They all broke up in laughter and resumed serious discussion.

One morning the Guardians came to the battery city at dawn and found all the hens had died of stress and boredom. Out in the barnyard a hen cocked her head on one side as she pecked among the gravel for specks of corn. "Quiet in there, isn't it?" she said. Somewhere, out in the primeval forest, a splendidly coloured cock rose on his talons, flapped his wings, stretched his strong neck and fiercely crowned head to the sky, and crowed three times to greet the sun. No one heard.

ACKNOWLEDGMENTS

I could not have written the above without the kind assistance of the Nobel Foundation, the Gulbenkian Foundation, the H. F. Guggenheim Foundation, the Rockefeller Brothers Foundation, the International Federation of Institutes for Advanced Study, and numerous other generous and well-meaning organizations dedicated to understanding "modernization."

POSTLUDE: CONFERENCE ODE

We had this conference   you see
to set the sorry world to rights—
to frame a new philosophy
It lasted thirteen days and nights

Exhausted   in our final round
officially we failed to find
a single plot of common ground
We were of a divided mind

We sought the one eternal truth
on which to base our polity
We slowly passed from age to youth
from wisdom to frivolity

Our days   so boring   soon became
merely a prelude to our nights
Sagacity served to inflame
a lust for frivolous delights

The darkness   brighter than the day—
while not producing something new—
had   Mr Chairman   this to say
One thing is certain: People screw

WHAT THE HUNTER SAW

How could they be so slender   men and girls?
Breeders yes   but breasts so small   high pointed
child sucks on what   swinging at waist   how feed?

Dragging spear butt   keeping low   in the juniper
bushes   mouth open   thirst   tangled greasy hair
flecking his eyes   raw dried meat
sundried   dirty   hanging at waist

NOTE: I have cheated here since Shanidar dates from approximately sixty-thousand years
ago and the young man in question could not therefore have seen Ur or any of the early
neolithic towns. But it is the contrast that matters, and that is still valid. Fables do not have
to respect chronology.

eyes flicker to berries   question   habit
dying hard   like him   near death   resisting

Last run   last rains   last hunt   kin dead
leg useless   blood dried   days gone   pain
loss   rains   no stars   rains   then heat   scorch
lost   more pain

How could they?   Girls like
unblooded boys   How could they be so slender?
Buttocks shrunk smooth   no use for child work
not the making or releasing   hips
chipped down like flints   brittle sounds
like falling ice at ankles and wrists   pieces
of shining ice   Men and girls   slender like
gazelles

All senses leap now   tell   urge
get up-wind   keep low   let Morg and Gmask
creep   creep deep in dust behind   then rise
and yell and watch the sentinel stot   stot
his up-and-down   useless   brave signal   Then
throw   stop the grace dead there in dust
grace into meat   young fed   mate pleased   night good
All lost   Morg to the tusks   Gmask in the rain

These human graciles laugh   move hand in hand
half naked   yes   skins   not wearing skins
cobwebs   from spider   giant   in their cave
spinning out the purple   violet cobwebs
And the ice that tinkled   tinkled   how
did it stay whole in heat of summer   how?
Laughter like breaking ice and song and
bird sounds   mating bird calls   coming
from beaks of males but not like beaks
moved from mouths to laugh and kiss the
slender girls

Moving now towards their
cliff   square   regular with square holes

in its sides   and trees   regular trees
two-sided   linking branches   leaning against
cliff
      Moving slowly through high yellow grasses
passing smaller   heavier   men and girls
cutting   stooping   curved knives   flint yes
but curved like new moon   useless for killing
brittle for hunt   break in flesh
                    Why hunt
the yellow   tall   seed-heavy   waving grass?

Stopping   all stopping   quiet eyes turned down
presence of power   sensed   strain   see a straggle
no   too regular   lines and lines these graciles
lines and lines   song   all regular   all
shaman chant   but hundreds   hundreds   how
to feed so many?
              Cobwebs   white   on old males
of herd   yellow   glinting like the grasses
round necks and foreheads   Green   yellow knives
at waist   Smooth lines   not gut   not creeper
dragging beasts   White bull   black ram   fat
clumsy   smooth   easy kill   one thrust   Chant
low   long   nearer   now in circle at flat rock
All eyes down   the graciles kneel   unknown
fear   bull   ram   but not of hills   plains   smooth
fat   people slender   beasts smooth   fat   stupid

Blurs now   not clear   sweat   tiredness   stay
hidden   hide spear   leg dead   body dying
but the hunt   hunt was good   Morg died well
Gmask lost in rains   Women   women heavy bellies
long breasts   huge buttocks   good women   waiting
at cliff base   wet   afraid   some others   yes
perhaps   women fertile   would be taken
Mnag's clan perhaps   too late
              Look   look again
last look   how did they stay so slender
the young ones   and their cliff   blurring out there
sticking like outcrop from dry plain

regular like leaning trees   like slender
lines of water through the grass   There were
no lines like that but men made them   yes
and white beasts   they made them   yes
and yellow grass   they made it   yes
and cut it down and made what?   what
did it matter now world was theirs
now
       Hills blur   hills theirs too in time
water for the grass comes from the hills
White bull dies from yellow knife
Fat ram dies from knife of ice
Graciles sigh together like lovers   mutter
one response to bloody shaman's cry
Then the stench   burning   flesh burning   blood
not for food   burn to burn   blood   flesh   fire

In all that death he felt his own   began
to sing his death song   nasal high   sending
to hills   sky   plain   herds   all the listeners
beyond   beneath
                 The graciles hear   freeze
horror   surround   horror   hiss   sacrilege
surround
            Feral one   hill brute   filthy thing
surround   close   stab   crawl   stab   roll   stab

Blood closes eyes   laughter   clinking ice
How could they be so slender   still give birth?

They left him for the buzzards   but at dusk
the women came and took him to the hills

Human self awareness is unique
in that we give voice to it through speech
Animals communicate but not
on existential questions   Language is
more than mere communication   it
admits of self reflection . . .

. . . not enough
to be a creature conscious of one's own
existence   one must be aware of one's
awareness and articulate the same

OVERHEARD IN THE PUB

"We'd start wi' the Jews   because they ask for it
I mean   if they'd shut up about themselves
and keep out of the way   they'd be alright"

"Yer right mate   First the Jews   Another pint?"

"Thanks mate   and then the Krauts   because they done
the Jews—which was their right—but still
they're dangerous bastards   so we'll do them next"

"Who then mate?"

                          "Well   I think the bloody Frogs
because they're bloody awful and because
they'd do us all if they 'ad 'arf a chance"

"Quite right mate   Get the filthy Frogs   Who then?"

"The blacks of course   the bloody lot because
they're   well   a bloody big embarrassment
worse than the Yids   They clutter up the place
You don't know where you are"

                          "Right mate   Not like
the old days eh?   'Ere   'ave another pint"

"Good on yer cobber   Then we'll get the Yanks
the fuckin' know-alls   serve 'em right   and then
the bleedin A-rabs and the little Chinks
and all the nasty little yellow men
What fuckin' use are they?"

"Right on mate—what?
That's what I asks myself   what fuckin' use?"

"No use at all   They hate our bloody guts
So we'll do them   and then the Indians
No more stupid voices serving chips
We'll choke 'em on their own chapatis   then
we'll finish off the Ruskies before they
blow us to bloody bits"

"The bloody bastards   right
An' all their pals   They would   Another pint?"

"Right 'o   Then all the Spicks and Wogs and Turks
and all the bloody rest   The Irish first"

"Right   Get them murderin bastards right up front
Who's left?"

"The friggin upper classes mate"

"That's right   the bleedin' middle classes too"

"And all the prolo-bloody-tariat
The lazy bleedin' bastards"

"Right   That's them
Who's left?"

"Just you and me mate   and I'm not
all that bloody certain about you."

EVOLUTIONARY POETICS

It's all too much.

The Beatles, *Yellow Submarine*

Consciousness out of context   (Muse I sing)
The point's been made before   change is too fast
The Neolithic revolution was
somewhat too fast for hunters   but they coped
The urban revolution was a jolt
but one that was absorbed and staggered by
with mere elaborations   nothing new
(Unless the sinister emergence of
a literate class which soon began to take
its literacy further than the lists
of punishments and tribute and supplies
and valedictions of pathetic kings
into the exploration of itself—
the fascination of the words and wordy
that was a revolution in itself
but did not make its impact fully felt
until the mass of men caught the disease)

But noting this and passing on we find
th'industrial revolution in degree
more of a jolt   even a jolt in kind
A rebirth   sudden   from the chrysalis
of mercantile and feudal caterpillar
into the fragile butterfly of steam
of coal and iron   capital and wealth
drawn not from land but from the sweated arms
of proletarians—peasants without land

and lacking all the certainty that dirt
between the fingers gives if it's *your* dirt
and not the filth that cannot be removed
because the skin is stained in laboring
for surplus value
                              That was change enough
into a different kind of slavery
But there had been so many slaves before
Why was this worse?   Because it held the seed
of anger different from a slave revolt
of possibilities beyond the dreams
of Spartacus or Christ—the dreams of Marx

(Continuing the theme of consciousness
out of context   but reflecting on
its wobbly route to this plateau   herewith
reflections on the crucial stages of
hominid history   Thus each stage produced
a curious "surplus" which somehow became
the basis   accidentally   for the next
"Preadaptation" in the jargon but
that hints of teleology   far too
deliberate a process   this is not
even a hint at dialectic   there
is struggle but no synthesis   At best
it's happy accident   So sorry Karl)

TREES

CIRCA 72
MILLION
YEARS B.P.

       Imagine if the rudimentary
primates had not made *that* cute excursion
Then goodbye grasping hand   binocular
vision   diminution of the sense
of smell etcetera*
   Surplus: "Intelligence surplus"
You didn't have to be that smart
to live in trees   It came in handy though

* By this time there had been a revolution
unseen yet terrible   the creatures dreamed

REM sleep is something unreptilian
it comes with mammals   With it comes the chance
of long-term storage in the memory
and hence the freeing of cells cortical
for other and more sinister endeavors
In lower mammals dreaming is enslaved
to theta rhythms   keeping it on rein
to those activities the species has
found useful in survival   But comes man
and like the other higher primates frees
his dreams from theta and dependency
on mere survival . . .

31

BIPEDALISM

CIRCA 5–6
MILLION
YEARS B. P.

                    and the striding walk
converted shambling brutes into efficient
machines for covering long distances
with minimal effort   You could not outrun
the prey   but you could walk the buggers down
What's more it freed the hands from locomotion
and hating idle digits as he does
Lord Belial quickly found them other work*
    Surplus: "Energy surplus"
You didn't have to be quite that efficient
to get by in the scramble for the meat
But what a great stride forward for mankind!

* and from this work man made himself   at least
so Engels would maintain   *The Part Played by
Labor in the Transition from Ape to Man*
(written in 1876 but only
published in 1896   those hands
were busy keeping Karl from penury)

HUNTING

I mean in earnest   Kill the beast
and organize the hunt and distribution
of meat within the horde   It came on slowly
perhaps at first   but once they got the point
then they were off and running   Yet the hunt
itself was maybe less important than
the organizing and the sharing   but
the meat made all the difference at that *
    Surplus: "Protein surplus"
You don't need the massive   (not that massive)
input of protein—those amino acids
that niacin   that vitamin B_{12}
But once you've got them then the bulging brain
and even more efficient striding walk
are poised for takeoff scarcely dreaming where

* A lot of effort currently is put
into the proof that "man the hunter" was
"man the scavenger"—a lazy lout
a carrion eater   robber of the kills
of more efficient carnivores   But think
the great decani of the hunt   the wolves
only attack the young   the old   the maimed
and lions steal from other hunter's kills
Now would our enterprising ancestors
have been less capable than wolves or dogs?
So if they drive these hunters from their prey
garnering a banquet second hand
they only imitate the lion   One small step
and they too could be pulling down the sick
A scavenger by any other name . . .

LANGUAGE

? PERHAPS
CIRCA 1
MILLION
YEARS B.P.

       Above all the talk
and permanent attachment of the memories
that could then be transmitted and preserved
passed slowly   surely on through song and verse
and myth mnemonics   proverb   formula
   Surplus: "Information surplus"
You didn't need that massive a change
in information processing   But on came speech
and names and sentences *   The angular
gyrus has a lot to answer for
But once you had   the brain was off and running
in circles more and more of its devising
Not circles in the world but strange recursive
pathways inside thought itself   thought about
thought about the thought of thought—the prospects
were alarming   This was the mother lode

* There are thase wha say Neanderthals
cannet be credeted weth "lengage" Wha?
Thar laranxes cad enle farm twa vawels
What thenk ye ef thes nefty argament?

AGRICULTURE

Why bother? No one's yet explained
why happy hunters having so much fun
would willingly exchange their affluence
for dawn to dusk back-breaking servitude
to mutant grasses   cultivated roots
The entire episode makes little sense *
Don't blame the brain   we had that long before
Some blame the women   (others think to credit
the female sex with this "great innovation")
Chacun à son goût   I'm with the hunt
  Surplus: "Food surplus"
and all its charming consequences
including leisure classes creaming off
their very own dear surplus from the mob
Chiefs   states   empires   wars and tyrannies
but above all . . .

* One theory that I like is that this step
was taken by the *least successful hunters*
Driven from the choicest hunting grounds
they turned to seeds and roots extensively
and since they were dependent found a way
to make their vegetarian supply
a great deal more reliable than that
of simple gatherers   If this isn't true
it ought to be   the irony is perfect

POPULATION EXPLOSION *

CIRCA 7
THOUSAND
YEARS B.P.

We were enough   We didn't
need so many   What do more mouths add
but hunger?   We are too alike each other
for numbers to do more than multiply
monotony   But given all that went
before it was inexorable
  Surplus: "Labor surplus"
Once you've got 'em keep 'em all employed
If worst to worst should come they can construct
your tombs and pyramids and temple courts
(after they've fought your wars and tilled your fields)
where that surplus information can
find outlet through the excess energy
and so to further cumulation . . .

* The human population had been stable
throughout the paleolithic at about
a million   Come the neolithic then
it shot up to a hundred million
Four billion later that might not seem much
but then it was a crowded little world
to those who had to cope so suddenly

WRITING

CIRCA 3–5
THOUSAND
YEARS B.P.

    Not enough to have
the language that you did not need   you choose
to make the symbols permanent and join
vision and speech in altering the brain
which surely had enough to occupy it *
   Surplus: "Concept surplus"
Goodbye old oral world for now we have
the anal institution of the pen
Science mathematics measurement
and records—above all those wretched files
And so to that appalling consumation
the growth of rational bureaucracy

(Between the first city states and the late
eighteenth century nothing happened.   Then . . .)

---

*Thus literate aphasics rarely make
more than a small recovery of speech
while their illiterate counterparts do well
and often speak as well as ever since
their brains are not encumbered with the need
to make the auditory-visual
connection   Literacy we take too much
for granted in its benefits   Why not
let's wait and see . . .

INDUSTRY

          So we return to where we are
and pick up the crazy   unforseen
consequences   patchworks   bits and pieces
serendipitous and accidental
cumulation of surplus upon surplus
rolling like a golem to its end
     Surplus: "Physical energy surplus"
leading God knows where
If we didn't need the brain   the hands
the walk   the meat   the words   the weeds   the crowds
the letters   surely we don't need the power
to exploit the energy of energy itself
Unhappy ape   You know not what you do
But driven from one surplus to another
you pile up problems that your cunning brain
was never meant to solve however well
it handles things mechanical*

So what?   This latest surplus helps you churn
the rate of change beyond the brain's capacity
to comprehend   much less control
The paradox of . . .
To say nothing of computers and nuclear
weapons   We could go on about those too
But I don't want to go on
I want to hear the Beatles singing
"It's all too much"

This was to have been a learned article
(". . . should like to introduce the concept
of the 'preadaptive surplus' as a useful

*   a surplus too
another preadaptive accident
that came from some severe selection for
manipulative skills   The brain is quite
obsessed with hands and feet as much as words

analytical tool which . . .")
It was all about how NATURE must win in the end
That's the way to bet but I
won't be around to collect

TWO MORE LYRICS
(to explore a few more things)

nempe aliae quoque sunt; nempe hac sine
viximus ante;

Lucretius, *De Rerum Natura* 4.1173

. . . .

THE SPIDER AND THE HAWK

I had not thought that it would end like this
And will I ever learn from my mistake?
Or learn from everyman's mistake—that bliss
is just for sleepers   pity those who wake?

For sleep of love is sleep of reason too
where dreamy madness weaves a dusty web
And therein I was trapped for love of you
watching the sluggish tide of wisdom ebb

Such sweet exhaustion   rocking in the wind
of all our fantasies each cloying hour
while madness   smiling like a saint that sinned
stared at the love-meal   waiting to devour

The fierce arachnoid pleasure of the bite
that sent the poison singing through my veins
I loved   as Tristan and Isolde might
have loved the potion surging to their brains

If only madness were complete I'd stay
asleep from reason   but in dreams a crack
of fretted logic filtering in the day
shows nightmare reason poised for the attack

He hovers with his cold hard empty eyes
(for reason takes no pleasure in his task)
and draws me from the web of my demise
until   awake   I see you in the mask

The multi-featured mask that madness makes
that once in dreams was love personified
but grins its vampire grin when one awakes
and screams the message   "Fool   your dreams have lied"

That sad old king was wise who never drank
and who was never mad because he knew
what I now know   with only dreams to thank—
I must love reason as I once loved you

LE PRINCE COCHON

I did not really want to be a beast
a prisoner in this skin against my will
yet when my long imprisonment has ceased
a beast I will be   and imprisoned still

You tell me that true love is my release
and I will love you true to gain reprieve
but time will come when truest love will cease
when I shall not rejoice   but you will grieve

My love is true   but not eternal truth
if what is finite ends is that a sin?

NOTE: Stories of the pig prince (or Marcasin) flourished towards the close of the seventeenth century in France. I am thinking in particular of those by the Comtesse de Murat, and the Comtesse d'Aulnoye.

41

Your love will last   mine not outlive its youth
I did not cheat   but still you cannot win

Your one true love will fade as you grow old
my love will be renewed at every feast
I shall grow sleek   emancipated   bold
and frightened as a poor imprisoned beast

Which of us suffers most is hard to tell
you reap a hard reward you did not earn
but each time Love unlocks my bestial cell
She leaves the door ajar for my return

Human consciousness is then defined
as consciousness of being conscious couched
in Language   The articulation of
awareness of awareness

This release
from our entrapment in the material base
is our first paradox   For the release
results in a more baffling enslavement
to language   in itself no less material
since anything expressed in it becomes
an object in the world incorporated
into the tissue of the brain through memory
What is expressed in language thus becomes
an object of the thought that's born of speech
Thus the expression of consciousness becomes
an object of that consciousness.

VIOLENCE:RITUAL::POWER:AUTHORITY

How many divisions has the Pope?

Joseph Stalin

....

Who would question that Man is the most intelligent of animals? No sensible person given Man's own definition of his intelligence.

Who would question that Man is the only animal with culture? None save those who regard potato washing or termite picking as cultural activities, which is simply to confuse "learned" with "cultural" (i.e. couched and transmitted in symbols). Even pigeons, tape worms and blood cells can learn.

Who would question that only Man has the necessary ingredient for this high intelligence and culture—language? None save those who play the Clever Hans with puzzled chimps.

No. We are the epitome, and though, in academic circles, souls are suspect, culture, language and intelligence are safe. What totters, teeters, and reels under the impact of modern science, though, is the nineteenth-century certainty that these automatically meant progress: inevitable, upward and onward, to the empyrean of utopian perfectibility in technologically superior, socially harmonious societies. Somehow the old Adam seems to have the last laugh and all these vaunted attributes are more easily put to the service, it seems, of the lesser instincts, the "animal" passions. The dinosaurs could no doubt have used their size for noble purposes had they known what these were. They did not, and they died out: we do, and are in danger of extinction.

The dismal truth has slowly dawned during the terrible twentieth century—the century of mechanized, bureaucratized extermination—that

43

culture, language, symbolic thought, intelligence, and the perfection of reason lead only to the technology of destruction, the cultivation of genocide, the intelligent organization of mass hysteria, and the rationality of cold war politics and hot war deaths.

So where's the catch? Must we drag in metaphors? Weight and size were perfect for the dinosaurs, until conditions changed and they fell over and died.* Culture and reason have worked beautifully for us—but we changed our own conditions, and we totter toward destruction. Reason does not motivate, and we do not understand our motivations—we follow them. Reason is the handmaiden of the passions: cold and indifferent in her servitude. The flaw is that we cannot reason well. We fear a slave revolt. The handmaiden must grovel.

But to what? To fanaticism, to conviction, to outrage, to righteousness, to the conviction of truth, to moral certainty. Those who cry against the curse of conviction piss into the wind of certitude. We are the best, but lack all conviction—since to be convinced would be to be fanatic. So we encompass our own demise.

So this is the catch? Yes, simply this. And now, to demonstrate its ultimate futility, I shall embark on a rational enterprise. Unlike the dinosaurs, we know what we are doing. So why don't we do something constructive? Well, we've really only just found out. Since Darwin. And we don't like what we know. For what we know is this: all that exalts us above the animal state is a superior capacity for self-deception. We call this culture, reason, intelligence, foresight, symbolic communication, etc., etc. We are born, digest, reproduce, grow old, and die like animals. And that of course is all there is to it. But the animals get on with it. A cruel God gave us only one thing more: the capacity to ask why, knowing there was no answer, but knowing that this capacity to ask for one would keep us busy and drive us crazy.

We invent incredible fantasy structures to justify our getting on with it (in one way rather than another) and call these cultures. We have even taken to inventing armies of people to investigate these alternative delusions and rationalize them. We are the masters of illusion. Magicians fascinate us; our hero is the con man. We invent the great con man in the sky to mastermind the greatest illusion of all: that we need not die. And aiding and abetting all this is the prime agent of rationality, the brain, whose major function is to protect us from reality so that we might act and not drown in endless processes of unresolvable decision-making.

---

* O.K. So they died from a nuclear winter following a meteorite strike. The principle is the same. Pick another extinct species. Ninety percent of all that have ever existed are extinct.

Well, now, the enigmatic title of this piece of self-destructive rationality is of course a take off on Lévi-Strauss's formula for formulas.* Violence is to Ritual as Power is to Authority. It isn't even true, but these two dimensions are part of a multifunctional, multidimensional, multifactorial analysis I choose to make so the hell with it. The problem is that violence and ritual are both found in nature; power and authority fall on another dimension that corresponds to nature and culture. But we started this whole game with violence, so reason demanded continuity and got her own unfortunate way. Try it again:

Nature:Culture::Power:Authority

Better. Violence and ritual cut across; they are yet another dimension/ factor. We can plot, as Lévi-Strauss saw, most things against the Nature:Culture dimension because it is our basic intellectual dichotomy and intellectual dilemma. Thus, for example:

Nature:Culture::Reality:Fantasy

makes good sense. Nature knows no fantasy. Of course for us fantasy becomes reality because our intelligence can make it such by restructuring reality according to our fantasies, as the sociologists of knowledge tell us at length.

To what should we oppose intelligence? Like Bergson I choose intuition, although this could be seen as intelligence working at high speed: computerized intelligence. But I will take it in a more old-fashioned sense and use intelligence to equal "reason" as opposed to "just knowing." But does:

Natural:Cultural::Intuition:Intelligence

really work? I think so, but a two-hundred page footnote on Bergson would be needed to justify it and that's another book, so let it pass. "Intelligence-intuition" is a continuum anyway, not an opposition, but the curious mix in us of both makes me think they are functions of the same process only seemingly different in their operation—and often not different at all in their outcome (viz the human versus the computer at chess). Leave it. But it matters. It is somewhere at the crux, for our

*Actually, I think it was Kant's in his *Prolegomena to Every Future System of Metaphysics that May Ever Arise in the Way of a Science* (1783)

central idea—our mother goddess—is imagination, which is the ultimate marriage of intelligence and intuition somewhere at the intersection of all these operations.

Let's try a few more since we still have space on our three-dimensional diagram. (I have to give this away: we are leading up to a diagram—the pictorially minded can take comfort.) Ritual and violence have to be a prime axis. Ritual is violence tamed, turned into fantasy: the rules of war at every level from domestic quarrels to SALT II agreements. Men love the diplomacy as much as the combat. The war of words is what matters for that is where true mastery lies in the realm of fantasy. And crossing this main axis is its equivalent at a more abstract level, for it represents how we interpret what is happening in a primate pack or a Versailles Conference: Power and Authority. Primates (and I single them out for snobbish reasons—they are well-connected) have Power: We have Authority. (Power is the ability to enforce one's will on others: authority is the right to do so. The ability is real: The right must be invented.) It is the supreme con game, authority. It is power either with or without force; an option no animal would understand. Those in authority often lack power completely. (Hence Stalin's sarcasm at the expense of the Pope.) Those in power often lack all authority: but they will kill you if you resist them. Democracies count heads and hand power to the numerical winner—he has no other. And this, among the other forms delineated so well by Max Weber, we call "authority" and we obey—more or less. No animal would be so riddled with reason, fantasy, intelligence, and culture. Tell him some small male has the vote and he will swipe the little animal aside. This done, a ritual baring of the gums will suffice to keep the upstart in his place. The ritual is a reminder of the reality of the swipe—of power. But authority is ritual fantasized: a game of rational make-believe. And because of this it is most fragile. There are those whose business is or can become the effective use of power, and for them authority lacks all authority if it is not enforced by bayonets or terror. Generals and Mafias overturn authority like the house of cards it is. But then they reinvent it: they claim the "people," or "respect" for cosa nostra, or the "public good," or whatever. They always had ritual—that goes with violence and really differs not that much from its animal counterpart: it is the reminder of the gun behind the smile. But authority they have to claim on some basis other than power. Even here though, "right of conquest" has been recognized as a basis for authority. But the heirs of the conquerors claim by right of inheritance, and so once again we are in the land of make-believe. And always out of the desert there is the possibility of the hairy figure with the staff striding in to claim his share of power on the authority of the God that speaks to him and not to priests and kings or elected representatives. "Zadok the priest *and* Nathan the prophet anointed Solomon king." (Italics mine.) Our willingness to submit to authority is purely human. Our pleasure and terror in seeing it overthrown by power, and the exercise of power through force itself, is part of the pre-cultural heritage that knew no fantasy and had only ritual to curb the excesses of power.

I throw in Hedonic:Agonistic. Why? Because Michael Chance's distinction serves, as does the one between ritual and violence, to show the mechanisms that lie behind our capacity for far-reaching self-deception. It is a dimension that suggests that even in the chimps (for example) the capacity for authoritarian delusion must exist. Dominance is agonistic (among baboons for example) when society is maintained by brute force translated into ritual. The hedonic society on the other hand can make pure display a mode of seizure of power—I almost said authority and there's the point. The animal with the most spectacular and effective display need not be the one that could, in open combat, lick the others. But they defer to what appears to be a demonstration of superior might. Reality:Fantasy begins here. We are its supreme elaborators. No kings, no mandarins (for all their poems), no aristocrats had authority without force in the last analysis. Yet for centuries they could wield authority with only a minimal show of force in many cases and virtually none in others. A fantasy of "superior birth" was enough. Other fantasies have succeeded, but they are fantasies none the less.

No analysis of modes of production, ecological adaptations, culture change, or social functions even gets to the starting gate unless it can deal with this primitive given about the human being: its capacity to accept authority however bizarre; its willingness to play out the make-believe, its weakness for the con man and his game.

And for the paradox: we have no option. We can only live by self-delusion. And by it we must perish. It is, in evolutionary terms, the size of the dinosaurs. And yet we call it reason.

I throw in Primate:Human for obvious reasons (using primate again to mean "non-human primate"). The glimmerings of our own idiocy are there in primates. But the primates escape the worst ravages. (They mostly encounter these at our hands.) And, courting screams of outrage, I offer Female:Male. Yet consider. This puts the female (human) close to nature where she obviously belongs. It makes her hedonic, realistic, powerful, intuitive, and natural by definition. Oppose her to the male whose intelligence is used for fantasy, authority, culture, agonistic struggle, and the dubiously human. What woman would wish to ape a man? Forgive my puzzlement at those who claim that all they want is to be better at the games of self-delusion than the illusion-riddled males. They can do better than that surely. Am I the last romantic feminist? But where is imagination? Somewhere hidden in the hinterland between intuition and fantasy, violence and culture, hedonic display and the pretentions of intelligence. Imagination is dead center and is ignored mostly because people fly to the poles, and polar opposites attract.

My Egri Bikaver is finished. All I can leave you is the multidimensional (inadequately represented in three) and multi-factorial (work out the factors for yourselves) diagram. And these few thoughts.

On the human existential predicament. Very simple: it is this animal's capacity to imagine a predicament. It is the problem of being able to ask, "why?" about existence. The existence is no problem. We exist in the same way all other animals exist and we do not ask why *they* exist. Nor do they ask it of themselves. We can ask *how* they—or we—came to exist, and the question is in principle answerable. But neither we nor they ask *why* they exist, because they cannot ask it of themselves, and only an animal that can ask the question qualifies for it. Even of so close a cousin as the chimp—very intelligent, very human—we do not ask it. Chimps are born, grow, eat, cavort, struggle, mate, make little chimp replicas, and die. This makes them no different from any other animal (at base than any other organism). The chimp does not ask why it exists, neither should we. We too are born, grow, eat, cavort, struggle, mate, make little human replicas, and die. We are no different. But consider: endow the chimp with one extra capacity—the capacity to ask why it exists? To ask what is its purpose? To ask how should it live? In other words to question its existence: its manner of existing. Nothing has changed. It is born, grows, etc., etc., and eventually dies. Nothing has changed. There is no more meaning now than before. But now it can ask "Why do I die? Why am I alive at all?" That is all. No more meaning. No change in its life—other than the questioning.

And that is us: chimps with existential questions. And yet the change is radical, because we then devote as much of our energy to answering or avoiding the question as the chimp did to eating, mating, etc. (Even those existentialists who agree that there is no meaning—for whatever

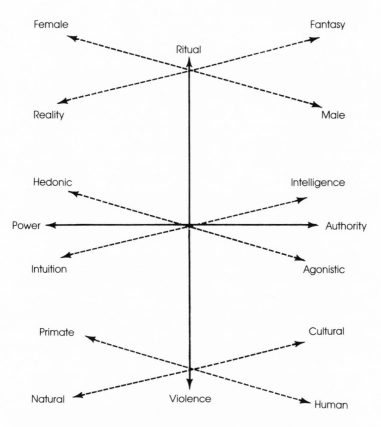

Female — Fantasy
Ritual
Reality — Male

Hedonic — Intelligence
Power ← → Authority
Intuition — Agonistic

Primate — Cultural
Natural — Violence — Human

Imagination is the (potential) integrating force of all these factors

reason—agree equally that we should hurry to invent some of our own.)
If there is an answer to such a non-question as "Why do I exist?" perhaps
it should be, "to ask that question." For that is all that has been added to
the tedious list—the capacity to ask why the list should be there at all. It
does not supply the answer. Without the capacity to ask we would still
exist; go through the paces as our ancestors did before they could ask it.
And we would likely survive and replicate well enough. (Or not; nature is
careless of species.)

So much for the human existential predicament.

O philosopher! O theologian! Try looking an intelligent chimp in the eye and asking "Why do you exist?" You will receive the only appropriate answer; your indifferent respondent will go off to eat, struggle, mate, make little chimp replicas, and die.

On the end of civilization. When civilization ends it will be the work of crazed saints and sober scientists; it cannot be saved by spaced-out musicians or drunken poets.

The violent imagination will triumph and will fail at one and the same time; we have no choice but to be human.

> And did some sly malicious god
> when an ape first stood and faced the sky
> prepare a two-edged gift   a rod
> it thought to cure this hubris by?
> It did   and so the creature choked
> then straining through its tears it croaked
> the first   pathetic   "why?"

TWO (More) GHOSTS ARE INVOKED

. . . .

LOVE AMONG THE PLANETS: BALLAD FOR THE GHOST OF YEATS

Where does love go in autumn
remembering the spring?
To the inner rings of Saturn
where no songs are sung

Where does love go in winter
yearning for summers gone?
Where all lost lovely things must go—
the dark side of the moon

Where does love go at midnight
with thoughts of golden dawn?
To Jupiter's cold darkness
where tired souls lie down

Where does love go at twilight
with memories of noon?
To Mercury's cruel surface
where all hopes burn

Where does love go forever
when planets cease to spin?
Where all things shall end their sorrow—
the deathfire of the sun

DIVINA COMMEDIA
FOR BYRON'S GHOST

The saga of belonging
is a comic tale of grief
where the days are full of longing
but the nights bring no relief

Where the dread of deep desiring
makes indifference a gain
but where loss and love conspiring
make the victory seem in vain

Where the tyranny of needing
makes parting a reprieve
but has separation feeding
a hunger to retrieve

Where the fierceness of possession
makes losing a release
but provokes an intercession
to restore possessive peace

Where the thousand ways of holding
are the shackles forged from greed
and the arms that are enfolding
do not strengthen but impede

Where every tense restriction
is a necessary theme
and each tedious interdiction
sets the limits of the dream

Where imprisoned in the dreaming
we are nervous but secure
and escape is but the scheming
to make surety more sure

For the tragedy of passion
is a comedy of fear

which the gods delight to fashion
in which mortals can appear

Where the gaining or the losing
leaves us weeping on the stage
in confusion freely choosing
both the exit and the cage

. . . recursive
Consider that for Hegel God was thought
thinking about itself*   For us then God
and human consciousness are one   This is
paradox the second   it makes God
an accidental consequence of His
creation

*As it was for that matter with Aristotle and Aquinas, the lat-
ter writing "Est in Deo intelligente seipsum Verbum Dei quasi
intellectus."

If recursive consciousness
depends on language as a necessary
condition of existence   then the same
is a contingent product   It need not
—like language—ever have evolved at all*

* The empirical issue here is not our concern. All we need to know
is that language occurred late in hominid evolution as a result of
structural developments in the left temporal lobe, the angular
gyrus, and the pre-frontal cortex. These, like any other evolved
features, need not have occurred. The rest of the animal kingdom
exists well enough without them, and the plant and inorganic
kingdoms lack them—even the rudiments of them—and survive
very well indeed. Or did so until the superior hominids took over.

THE INTERROGATION:
A Nightmare

> *You must remember that in these proceedings*
> *things are always coming up that are simply be-*
> *yond reason, people are too tired and distracted to*
> *think and so they take refuge in superstition. I'm*
> *as bad as anyone myself. And one of the supersti-*
> *tions is that you're supposed to tell from a man's*
> *face, especially the line of his lips, how his case is*
> *going to turn out. Well, people declared that judg-*
> *ing from the expression of your lips you would be*
> *found guilty, and in the near future too.*
>
> Franz Kafka, *The Trial*

. . . .

Standard scene. Court in session. At a long, raised table the inquisitors in dark suits and darker shadow. In front of them the prisoner in a harsh spotlight. Behind, coughs and mutterings indicate a small audience. One black-suited figure in a large chair at the center of the table speaks.

COURT: Have you anything to say before we pass judgement?

PRISONER: But there hasn't been a trial yet, has there?

COURT: (*Surprised*) You do not think that the evidence of your life, work, and opinions is enough to condemn you?

PRISONER: Maybe. But doesn't justice have to be seen to be done—or something like that?

COURT: (*Sighs*) Very well. We must go through with a formal trial if the prisoner wishes it.

PRISONER: He sure as hell does. Of what is he accused?

54

COURT: There is no accusation. This is an enquiry into your fitness to be a member of society. There is a prima facie case that you are not. We shall question you.

PRISONER: This court is, I hope, ruled by arbitrary standards of law and procedure?

COURT: Why do you ask that?

PRISONER: Because, if so, this trial becomes a game with rules and I stand a chance.

COURT: No. Your answers will be judged solely on truth or falsity.

PRISONER: Then I am doomed, for no man knows the truth.

COURT: Indeed he does; the truth speaks for itself.

PRISONER: On the contrary, someone always speaks for it, and whoever has the voice has the veracity.

COURT: Be assured The People will recognize the truth, for, by definition, what the will of The People recognizes is true, and we are the representatives of the will of The People.

PRISONER: No. The truth resides outside us. It is a small cruel eye that will not release us from its gaze—not you, not me, not The People, not their representatives.

COURT: You are doing your case no good by speaking blasphemy in your defense. The People will ignore your remarks. The inquisition will begin as of now. You will be asked questions about the epochs of Man's history and you will reply what you believe to be the truth. We shall question you in turn.

(He nods to the first dark figure at the far end of the line and the question and answer session begins. It is all quiet and reasonable. Almost a conversation.)

Q. Describe the Age of Innocence.

A. The Age of Innocence was when man killed without guilt, copulated without shame, and got drunk without either.

Q. What of the Dawn of Civilization?

A. This was when man left the State of Nature and discovered the Nature of the State. After which life became nasty, brutish, and short.

Q. Before this was Man a noble savage?

A. He was a human savage—noble and ignoble by turns.

Q. And the Rise of the State?

A. Was when man invented his most potent chain: the chain of office.

Q. And the Age of Matriarchy?

A. It was, by definition, the age when mothers ruled. Two other types were automatically killed: men, once their useful breeding life was over; women who were not mothers, and who aspired to be like men.

(This next came from an inquisitor who had a beard and deep-set eyes, but the light was not good enough to make out more than a faint Viennese accent.)

Q. What does a woman want?

A. A god to be the father of her children.

Q. What does she get?

A. Constant frustration when this has not materialized, or complete self-deception when she believes it has.

Q. Should men avoid investigation of this issue?

A. Certainly not. The unexamined wife is not worth loving.

Q. Will men ever be as gods?

A. Not while sober women make the assessment.

Q. And what of God?

A. One thing is certain: God cannot be as bad as his believers make him out to be.

Q. Is God dead?

A. More probably bored into silence.

Q. How then should men rid themselves of God?

A. Those gods whom men would destroy, they first make sad.

Q. And what do the gods do then?

A. They leave in the intermission.

Q. What is the greatest of man's gifts?

A. Self-deception: the power of delusion.

Q. Not reason?

A. Reason is its own kind of deception: all the more deluding since it claims the opposite.

Q. Does not reason control the emotions?

A. Reason is an emotion; an excess of emotion is madness; excessive ratiocination is its own kind of lunacy.

Q. Does not reason arbitrate among the emotions?

A. The emotions, of which reason is one, are not subject to arbitration. It is the war of all against all. The triumph of one emotion is madness.

Q. And if reason triumphs?

A. Then its form of madness will prevail.

Q. Which is?

A. Ratiocinosis: the delusion that reason is not an emotion and therefore can save us from the emotions.

Q. Are we all doomed to self-deception?

A. Yes, but we need not all work at it; we can delegate delusion.

Q. Must some of us always lie then on behalf of others?

A. As for lying, our savants can do that for us.

Q. What cure is there for the madness of reason?

A. For ratiocinosis? Only an inoculation by some other form of emotional madness.

Q. What do you suggest?

A. Imaginative compassion.

Q. Is that not rather terse?

A. Very well. If civilization as we know it should end it will be the work of crazed saints and sober scientists; it cannot be saved by spaced-out musicians and drunken poets. The violent imagination . . .

Q. Have we not heard all this before?

A. You should have listened the first time.

Q. To what end if reason is futile?

A. To the end of preventing boring repetition.

Q. Are you not being frivolous with the court?

A. The court is frivolous to start with since the verdict is predetermined.

Q. Do you accuse the court of prejudice?

A. No. Simply of mean-mindedness and murderous intent.

Q. Do you think that is our purpose?

A. The end justifies the meanness.

Q. Does anything justify bad puns?

A. Frivolous litigation might. Serious litigation certainly would.

Q. On what grounds?

A. Litigation is reason used to perverse ends—puns are the subversion of reason by using a rational linguistic process to make nonsense of the process itself. Therefore to use bad puns to annoy judges is to use reason to combat reason and provoke unreasonable outbursts.

INQUISITION IN CHORUS: Absolute bullshit!

PRISONER: Thank you for making my point.

JUDGE: The questioning is no longer serving any useful purpose . . .

PRISONER: I couldn't agree more.

JUDGE: Let us stay within our mandate to ask of the epochs of history. Continue.

Q. What was the Age of Enlightenment?

A. When reason was exalted over fact with a resulting constipation of the intellect.

Q. And the Age of Science?

A. When fact triumphed over reason and produced a diarrhea of the mind.

Q. What was the distinctive feature of the Age of Faith?

A. Hundreds of cathedrals claimed to have the phallus of Christ.

Q. Have we improved on the Age of Faith?

A. We no longer treasure the phallus of Christ; we promote the female orgasm.

Q. Do these have something in common?

A. They are both relics.

Q. What of the Age of the Common Man?

A. The age of the common man has only one notable achievement, the invention of new tort: Invasion of dignity.

Q. And the Technological Age?

A. When faith and reason will combine to destroy the fruits of their own folly.

Q. What then of the Age of the Individual?

A. It has witnessed the most obscene acts ever of collective violence and tyranny.

Q. Who shall inherit the Earth?

A. The Insects; they had the wisdom to abolish the individual will as a social force. We try hard to do so, but we have gone too far. We are like insects who behave as such except that we can be swayed by individual wills.

Q. What of the Age of Aristocracy?

A. When we ensured the incompetent would govern by reason of superior birth.

Q. And the Age of Democracy?

A. When we ensured that the mediocre would govern by reason of popular choice.

Q. And the Age of Socialism?

A. When we ensured that the unimaginative would govern by reason of their ideological purity and complete lack of scruple.

Q. What prevents the best from governing?

A. They lack the energy of will and singleness of purpose.

Q. Why do they lack this?

A. The best have only many good questions; the governors have a few bad answers; people prefer answers to questions.

Q. What of the Rise of Bureaucracy?

A. It ensures its own failure. It is intended for the governance of human beings, but the qualities demanded of a bureaucrat are of their nature inhuman.

Q. And the Age of the Proletariat?

58

A. The proletarian is a peasant without land. Deprived of land he lapses into a predatory existence. The proletariat is a pack.

Q. And the Capitalist?

A. Is the hunter who has become the hunted—even by his hounds, the bourgeoisie.

Q. And his response?

A. To form his own packs.

Q. And the Silent Majority?

A. Their silence is ignorance multiplied by fear and divided by indifference. They will fall between the packs—noisily.

Q. What of the Age of Revolution?

A. Revolutions cannot succeed, for if they do they are no longer revolutions.

Q. Even the Sexual Revolution?

A. It is the ultimate triumph of male chauvinism: countless females available with whom men can copulate while assuming no responsibilities whatsoever.

Q. What then of We, The People?

A. You are a pool of sulking sharks. Greed has you rending each other in short order.

(Much buzzing and consternation. The judges confer briefly with much nodding. They sit back.)

COURT: We declare that you have failed.

PRISONER: May I know the reason?

COURT: You have attempted to be too clever in order to demonstrate individual superiority. The People's truth being collective, it cannot allow assumptions of individual superiority, and so finds your testimonial untruthful.

PRISONER: But in so condemning me The People surely tries to show its superiority to me?

COURT: No. The People simply declares you its equal, and its condemnation is not superiority, merely justice.

PRISONER: Justice is man's easiest excuse . . .

COURT: You will not be allowed further testimony . . . excuse for what?

PRISONER: I was going to say for oppression, but that is so weak I risk a just condemnation.

COURT: You are in any case condemned. You will be taken from this place to a place of lawful reeducation where you will be washed by the brain until you be humble, and when you are in full possession of your popular senses you will be released to do useful work in a capacity that will fit your pleasant mediocrity: a mediocrity all the more worthy for having been achieved. The case is closed. The People will retire.

(One judge demurs and asks that the prisoner be recalled for an extra question. The court is annoyed but agrees.)

Q. Why do you despise The People?

A. I do not despise The People—rather people. I simply do not recognise a category of The People. The People is a mistake.

Q. Then whom do we represent?

A. You are people who probably represent other people. But not The People.

Q. What of the Historic Destiny of The People?

A. A collective delusion of some people.

Q. As with the so-called Chosen People?

A. One of the greatest collective delusions of all time, for of all people they are surely the most obviously abandoned.

Q. But do they not survive despite all persecution?

A. They do. But so do the Irish and they certainly don't think they were chosen.

Q. What have the Irish and the Jews in common?

A. They both believe that reality is chaos—only narrowly kept at bay.

Q. And how do they differ?

A. The Jews think they can do something about it.

JUDGE: I see no point in further questions.

(But the bearded one leans forward and asks one anyway.)

Q. We asked you what a woman wanted. What does a man want?

A. Someone to fuck, something to hate, and some way to forget.

Q. But what of . . .

A. Anything you want to add comes under the third head.

Q. To forget what?

A. Whatever.

Q. A strange answer from one who has not, as he expected, been sentenced to die but to live.

A. A sentence of life dissipates the mind abominably.

JUDGE: He is incorrigible. Remove him.

(All nod, All leave. Lights dim. Figures move . . .)

> Vishnu in his lotus-dreaming groaned
> and moved one shoulder slightly   Mountains fell
> Continents shifted   Empires collapsed
> Received ideas appeared ridiculous

To say full consciousness is accidental is
only to say it is a product of
natural selection   Everything
is such a product   This is not to say
that it is inexplicable   there must
have been selection pressures favoring it
most likely by the preservation of
those organs that had generated speech
Occuring as mutations their adaptive
value made for ultimate retention
within the pool of genes

                    Nevertheless
we face the startling prospect that the mind
being thus conscious will eventually
stumble on this simple lonely truth
after a history of monumental
efforts to use this consciousness to weave
the rich illusion of necessity

NOTE TO THE THEOLOGIAN
(as an afterthought to the foregoing reflections of the
philosopher of mind who somehow got in on this act)

If God is independent of our flesh
(not a by-product* but the primal cause)
God cannot help   Pure thought addressing thought
(perhaps consumed with curiosity
that matter could achieve the same result)
became incarnate in the Word made Flesh
and so experienced humanity
died at its hands   brooded three days   then fled
with vague assurances   (still unfulfilled)

It's not quite that Divinity is dead
it just abandoned the experiment
absconded to the safer sphere of thought
thinking about itself
                But maybe God
is haunted by the sojourn in the flesh
The independent Word that gave us form
is tainted by its own creation
                    Once
fear simmered only in the hearts of men
But since the incarnation there is fear
at the very epicenter of all being

* as in the philosopher's argument (vide supra)

Two

The
Trial
of
George
Washington:
Documents
in the
Case

HOW WE CAME BY THEM

· ·

LETTER TO THE PUBLISHER

Dear Ken,

Just before he died, Senator James Handler gave me the enclosed manuscripts. As you *do* know, I met him through Senator Fulbright; what you don't know is that we discovered, to our surprise, that his wife and I had an ancestor in common—my great-great grandfather—a Dublin lawyer and legal historian, Augustin Fox. I did not know the senator's son John very well. He was killed in Vietnam, as you also know. But before he left he gave his father the manuscript (his letter is enclosed). The senator did not think that he himself had long to live (he proved right) and given the odd family connection, (the relevance of which will become obvious on reading the stuff), and my contacts in the publishing world, he thought I would be the appropriate person to do something about it all.

I would suggest, in the first instance, just publishing it "raw" before letting the historians and other vultures get at it. It is so close now to the bicentennial of the notorious trial. Anyway, here are the photocopies, the rest is up to you.

As ever,

Robin

P.S. My otherwise rather pedantic ancestor refers to the "Duke of Wellington" making a speech "in the House of Lords" in 1811. At that time Wellesley was still only a Viscount and, I thought, in Portugal. So who's perfect?

LETTER FROM LT. JOHN BRIDGES HANDLER
TO HIS FATHER SENATOR
JAMES WHITMORE HANDLER

Fort Dix, N.J.
Dec. 12, 1970

Dear Dad,

This will be the last letter before I leave. I am allowed to tell you that I am at Fort Dix (which is no news) but nothing else, of course. I had said what I had to say in the previous letter—at least about how I felt, and you must have thought me ridiculously sentimental, but I meant it. Since Mom died I've felt closer, and we are all that is left of the "clan" now. But one more thing cropped up—something very strange, and you should know about it.

Just before she died, Mom gave me one of her treasured "heirlooms" (you know how she hoarded all that stuff from England—some junk, some antiques, some curios—but all precious to her.) Well, this was a plain, heavy, wooden box of no distinction (except its age!) It had a rusty lock and key that had obviously not been often turned. She told me to keep it until after she was dead. (She never flinched about dying did she?) She knew I might go to Vietnam and she asked me to look at what was inside before I went. It came to her, she said, from *her* mother— Grandma Bridges (who I met when I was little—I think—on one of those trips to see the English relatives, but I don't really remember.) It had "come down to" Grandma Bridges from her mother, and even perhaps from hers—I'm not sure, but her name was "Anne," and it was "Anne's box." (Mom was the keeper of the family history, of course, but you may *just* know who she meant.) Anyway, I was to read what was in it if ever I "decided to go off and die for my country" as she put it (as she *would* put it.)

Dad, it's the strangest thing. "Anne's" husband was evidently a legal historian, a retired lawyer, who lived in Dublin although he'd practiced law in England and had been something called a "Parliamentary draughtsman"—whatever that was. Anyway, he'd gotten hold of some fragments of *the actual record of Washington's trial!* Can you imagine? They seem genuine enough, and his covering note speaks for itself. He obviously meant it to be published, but for reasons I don't understand, "Anne" just locked it up and put it with his other stuff and never did anything about it. It was among the odds and ends that "came down" from mother to daughter I guess until it came to Mom. I think perhaps no one had even bothered to read it before her, and all she said to me was what I told you—except for that odd remark of hers about war and politics being "a comedy for male voices." To a son who was about to be a soldier and a husband who was a politician! Well. That was Mom.

Now I don't know what to do. I've read the whole thing and I see what she means. I don't want to re-hash our arguments, but now *I* am going off to fight in someone else's civil war when I don't approve of going or fighting—and because "my country" demands it. Or is it just the politicians who demand it to save their faces? I'm sorry. Oh. I'll go. I'm on my way. Like those English (our ancestors in fact) who went when they didn't want to go. It was their Vietnam, Dad. They didn't learn, neither have we. Washington had. You'll see what I mean when you read it. So I'm sending it to you. It's a gem, historically I mean. You'll know what to do with it. But I guess if I'd had a sister it may never have seen the light of day! Will we ever understand women? I meant what I said in the other letter Dad. I'm glad our last talk was by the Charles with the crews out and the leaves turning. I'll do my best and pray to God that we see each other before long.

Your loving son,
John

HANDWRITTEN MANUSCRIPT FROM THE BOX

Dublin 1861

"To hang George Washington was our worst mistake."

Every schoolboy knows these famous words of the Duke of Wellington in the House of Lords on the occasion of the granting of independance to the former American colonies in 1811 (to forestall another alliance with the French it seems.) That the government took the whole thing badly was expected, but it had decided to accept the inevitable. There was no way to retain the allegiance of the colonies without another costly and probably disastrous war like the one of 1775–81. It was true that technically Great Britain had "won" that particular struggle, but was there ever a victory so Pyrrhic, or damage done to crown and country so extensive? The Tories never recovered after North's fall from grace; the King's friends were pretty well discredited despite Charles James Fox's never-forgiven attempt to prop them up; the Whigs gained so rapid an ascendency that only the prestige of the Iron Duke himself held the Tories together in a semblance of unity and narrow probability of occasional governance—and this largely due to the fractious nature of the Whigs and their passion for factions.

All this is well enough known, but we lack very much reliable evidence of the signal event by which the crown so sadly miscalculated: the trial and execution of George Washington himself. The details of his final defeat at Yorktown are also well enough known but should perhaps be summarized.

The battered "American" army had hoped to bluff Sir George Clinton in New York by leaving four thousand men with bogus camps and even bakeries in New Jersey to suggest a long stay. This would keep Clinton and his sizable force locked up in New York where they felt safe among the Loyalists. (The brave Irish volunteers of the King's Loyal American Regiments had already staged, on the day of their patron saint, a march down the Broad Way in the city of New York. It has become a annual event I gather, although its origins are not much spoken of.) Meanwhile, Washington was to march to Yorktown and catch Cornwallis napping, forcing him into a seige. The French navy was to blockade the coast thus preventing relief for "the British" from the sea, and the French army under de Rochambeau (*not* de Lafayette as so many schoolboys insist with typical sloppiness) was to come through the Carolinas to Washington's support, thus bottling Cornwallis up at the end of the Yorktown peninsula. Faced with two armies in front and the French navy behind, he would be forced to surrender.

What exactly happened to wreck this admittedly brilliant plan is still confusing to historians, but some things are clear. Cornwallis received intelligence of the plan and warned Clinton, or Clinton perceived the bluff and warned Cornwallis, or spies of the American side got word to both. In any case, Cornwallis anticipated the joining of the two forces and moved his own, with a brilliant manoeuvre, between them. As far as we understand it, Washington (and his chief advisors Lee, Lincoln, von Steuben, and de Lafayette) saw this as a blunder in which Cornwallis would be trapped. But Clinton meanwhile had marched from New York, swept aside the four thousand surprised Americans with his own eighteen thousand men, and was marching on de Rochambeau's rear. There was still the French navy; but then disaster struck. Admiral de Grasse made the crucial miscalculation of the war, strung his ships out too far, and allowed the British fleet to cut his line in half, sink two of his ships and send the rest scuttling for the Indies.

Item: Washington was between the fleet and Cornwallis. Item: de Rochambeau was between Cornwallis and Clinton. Item: at that moment Cornwallis struck in the most brilliant stroke of a brilliant career: he attacked the French *centre* at exactly the time the fleet opened with a bombardment of the Americans from the sea. He cut the French in two and joined up with Clinton while the British bombardment kept the already exhausted and undersupplied Americans helpless.

The surrender was inevitable and was received by Brigadier (*not* General as most history books insist with typical lack of attention to scholarship) Charles O'Hara, since Cornwallis would not deal directly with rebels. However—and this became an important point in the trial it seems—he did allow them to surrender with full honours of war. One presumes that this was to avoid further foolish fighting on their part that, while ultimately futile, would have cost many British lives. Cornered rats fight the fiercest, as the popular saying has it. Cornwallis, in view of later events, has been naturally reticent about his motives in this matter, but he did proceed, properly, to arrest Washington and his officers and to round up as many of the rebel leaders as possible. (Franklin was safe in Paris, and a great number, led by the Rev. Mr. Witherspoon, rushed to renounce their former adherence and swear allegiance to the crown. This, again, Cornwallis wisely accepted and Lord Howe confirmed, although there were those who hurled unwarranted charges of "leniency" at them later as we know.)

Again, what happened back in London at the court is not as clear as it might be. Apart from some cautious letters between the King and Lord North—largely to do with the latter's health and the King's advice of "abstinence and water!"—we have little hard evidence and much of that is merely circumstantial or hearsay. (This has not prevented novelists, dramatists, journalists, and others from speculating wildly and with complete lack of respect for historicity of course.) What is certain from the outcome is that the King—on the advice of North and probably Thurlow (the violently anti-American attorney-general)—decided not to hold the trial in America (for what are surely obvious reasons); decided to hold it in London (where it could be better controlled); decided to try Washington

69

first (as an example); and decided to try him by special court martial rather than in a civil court (again for obvious reasons). The last move was on the surface a clever one, but almost, as we know, had the engineers hoist on their own petards (whatever they may be). Military men can be remarkably independent-minded, particularly when they have their peerages and are not looking for further promotion. But, despite the ravings of some Whig "experts," it was quite legal. The special act of Parliament was probably not even necessary. Washington was a commissioned Colonel of Militia (Virginia) and hence open to court martial for treason. But the act was easily passed in the aftermath of the collapse of the parliamentary opposition in the wake of the Yorktown debacle.

The question of the role of the aforementioned opposition is the subsequent events, and of Franklin's even stranger part in them—cloaked in his immunity as an accredited French diplomat—is the more tangled part of a most tangled tale. Their initial vociferous support for Washington; their equally precipitous withdrawal of same; their largely successful exploitation of public ambivalence over the execution—all suggest murky politicking of a questionable nature by men more concerned with political advantage than the rights and wrongs of Washington's case. But should we expect otherwise? Burke, of course, and the peers (Amherst, Dartmouth, Conway, Effingham) stood firmly and honourably by the beleaguered American as was consistent with their opposition to the war throughout. (We have every reason here in Dublin, and at Trinity especially, to be proud of Mr. Burke's totally honourable—if at times a little verbose—part in an affair where the English, and in particular my distant collateral relative Fox, played such a dubious role.) Again, in the Commons, Mr Barré was perhaps without blemish. (It is curious to me that his name should have been linked with that of the reprobate Wilkes in naming a town in Pennsylvania; but those were early days.) Wilkes in particular, and Fox with his talent for opposition and great hunger for office, played a curious and suspect part, the details of which will probably never be known. (Not that this prevents the wildest rumours being presented by so called popular historians as undeniable facts. Macauly has a lot to answer for. I allude chiefly to the ridiculous rumour that through the offices of Franklin, George Washington was actually conducted into the presence of His Majesty King George the Third of England; that the King offered him a "bargain": American independence— or at least all that was promised in North's "conciliation bill"—in return for a plea of guilty followed by a royal pardon; that Washington was persuaded by the radicals to refuse—with the terrible consequences that ensued. It is impossible to apprehend what the motives of the principals might have been in such a bizarre affair; but many believe it took place. Unfortunately, the King's madness, Washington's death, and Franklin's disappearance have obviated any possibility of ever knowing the truth. Tales of "hooded figures being taken from the Tower by night" are the stuff of popular fantasy, nothing more.)

For us, however, as historians of the legal process, the saddest lacuna of all is the almost complete absence of any record of the trial itself. The burning of the Houses of Parliament left us nothing but the charred remains of the only court record that had been allowed but had been locked away with a fifty-year secrecy clause by yet another of those convenient acts of Parliament that should not, but often do, bend if not actually break the constitutional process. The fact that there was, then, virtually no record has not prevented the various protagonists from being variously loquacious on the subject; but with the three military judges having been sworn to silence and now dead, the prosecution and defense counsel having killed each other in a duel, and the other witnesses differing so much in what they remember, only the records themselves can give us the unvarnished truth.

The court's summing up (which we shall append) was published of course; but as for the rest we have only these fragments—bits and pieces of the actual court record that escaped the flames and have only now come to light (through circumstances I cannot detail but in which my position as a former parliamentary draughtsman was not without consequence). Perhaps it is as well; we have been too close to the events until now to assess them with cool enough blood; but since, within the last year, the whole issue in another form has been revived with the unfortunate outbreak of hostilities between the "Union" and the newly described "Confederacy," it is perhaps timely to reconsider if we cannot learn from history.

Sympathy at the moment seems to be with the Confederacy; but we must ask ourselves, is their case at the bar of history any stronger than that of the colonies? Are we not in danger here of supporting so eagerly what we condemned so readily in 1782? Is armed rebellion against a duly constituted sovereign authority ever justified? And if so, for what reasons? Must we with the cynic agree that it is justified only if it prospers, for then "none dare call it treason"? And in what is essentially a civil war, what part should a foreign nation play? If we support the Confederacy are we not playing France to Mr. Davis's George Washington? These matters will continue to be debated. The trial of George Washington scarcely settles them. His remarkable closing speech—after, presumably on his attorney's advice, remaining silent throughout the trial—attests to a change of vision that his ordeal engendered. Perhaps there is time to learn from that?

But I stray from my task, and can only plead age and infirmity for these wanderings that are not relevant to our appreciation of the historical value and admitted veracity of the fragmentary records we have here. To straighten the record is our aim, and to this end a word must be said about the court and its principals.

The office of the Judge Advocate had appointed three military judges but had been careful not to pick any whose views were strong or controversial and who had been known to take any particular public stand on the issue of the rebellion. General the Earl of Thornton was Commander-in-Chief Northern Command, a sound officer, versed in military court procedure, known for his fair if severe conduct of trials. Major-General Lord Brooke was the most obscure of the three, and as one wag put it was only known to have strong opinions about recessing early for lunch. Sir George Campbell was the most interesting of the three. He had been knighted by King George II for his services against the Stuarts in '45, and presumably Thurlow at least assumed that all Campbells hated all rebels. Also, given the large contingent of Scots in the British forces, it was perhaps thought judicious to give them some representation in the court (or perhaps even to remind them of the awful consequences of rebellion for one last time). But Campbell was interesting. He was, as a result of his wounds, no longer on active service but was a very learned man, well read in philosophy and an admirer of Lord Kames. He had the very unmilitary habit of taking legal issues seriously, which must have caused the prosecution some bad moments even though they could have had no real qualms about the verdict.

I am forgetting, of course, the evidently spectacular appearance of Lord Cornwallis for the defense—on the pleas that "the rules of war having been observed, a de facto state of war did exist" and that Washington should be treated as a prisoner of war. It was, naturally, disallowed; but evidently the army (that is, Cornwallis) was furious at being made to stage a military trial. They—and I think in particular Howe, who had clung throughout his generalship to his opposition to the war and insisted on his role as "peace commissioner"—wanted none of it, and had assumed the civil arm would "do the dirty work," as Cornwallis is reputed to have said. But again we are drifting into hearsay. (Why *is* it so tempting?) Oh yes! It very nearly misfired!

The choice of prosecutor was brilliant. Colonel the Honourable John Hampshire was perhaps the best legal mind in the army, and certainly the *decanus* of cross-examiners. It is also rumoured that he had a passion for the conviction and death of Washington stemming from his friendship with Major André—the unfortunate young officer Washington felt obliged to hang for spying in the curious affair of Sir Benedict Arnold (of whom more later). Washington's motives were simple and even logical. He had to maintain that he was the commander of the army of a sovereign state, and André clearly was spying—he was in civilian dress for a start. Spies must be hung if the war is a legal war. So André had to die. But not one of the Americans—Washington included—wanted to hang this charming young officer (who was said to have been engaged to the young lady from Philadelphia who subsequently married Arnold! More and more curious)! However, Hampshire never forgave Washington, and although no great issue was made of this at the trial, it seems, the undertones can be seen occasionally in Hampshire's questions.

(How strange these human passions are. How irrelevant to our task of dealing with the history of jurisprudence. Yet their fascination for us is surely something that the science of man—if, as Lord Melbourne said, it be a science—should explore. I find Mr. Mill remarkably unhelpful on this score; less so than Bishop Butler; and Mr. Darwin is, I confess, too new for me to assimilate the possible revolutionary consequences of his claims to truth.) But again I wander. Tiredness afflicts me easily these days; but since I am the only person with these records I must put them in some order, edit them, explain as best I can, which is so little.

Yes. Fenway. Got as a civil counsel for Washington (quite proper in a military trial) by Wilkes and Fox presumably, with Franklin in the background, as usual. Strange man Franklin: eloquent but untrustworthy, brilliant but dissolute. No wonder he was fond of the radicals. And Fox and Wilkes—always at each others throats and yet conniving together when they saw advantage, as in exploiting Washington. Can it be that there is a special "race" (Mr. Darwin?) of these radical politicians who seem to have so much more energy than the rest of us and so little scruple? Or is this just age speaking? But I wander. No. Fenway was picked because he was *not* one of the radicals. He was in fact a nephew of Amherst, which gave him some Whig credentials but on the other hand also put him close to the army (at least the Ordnance Department). He evidently, according to those who knew him before his untimely death (so young) used often to tell the story of the queer Granville Sharp, clerk at the Ordnance Office, who spent his life trying to free negro slaves at the ports. (If they

73

spent one night—or was it two nights—on English soil they were legally free, I think. So he used to smuggle them off the boats, hide them, and rush them to court for a freedom order after two days.) Well, he had no fortune, no means, no patron, but he resigned from the Ordnance Office at the outbreak of the American hostilities because he wanted, as he said, "no part in this bad business." He was like so many—he was for Washington's acquittal but detested his keeping of slaves. "The yelps for liberty," said Dr. Johnson, "came loudest from the keepers of slaves." Hampshire says that somewhere in the trial as I recall. And now the proverbial chickens have come home to roost and the "free" keepers of slaves are fighting for "freedom" from the keepers of "free" America! Eheu! Eheu! But Fenway. Yes. Young. Yes. Brilliant. Less experienced, less cunning than Hampshire. My hand tires. The fragments are here. Ah yes, the prosecution.

It has been remarked, often with surprise, that it only produced two witnesses: The Massachusetts judge Jonathan Sewall, and, of course, General Sir Benedict Arnold, the hero. Why only two? There may have been other reasons, but one looms large: according to the treason act of King Henry VIII, only two were needed. That was all the law required: two witnesses that the accused had "made armed rebellion against the King in his realm; put himself at the head of rebellious forces; allied himself with the King's enemies; caused the King's justices to be slain . . ." and so on. (There is something in the act about "violating the King's consort and eldest unmarried daughter"—heaven knows why. Keen as they were to press the whole catalogue of charges, that one was, I believe, omitted, although "imagining the death of the King and the Royal Family" *was* left in. How on earth does one prove *that* for goodness sake?) Yes. Two witnesses.

The defense of course was out to prove that Washington's actions were *not* treason but self-defense against the crown (or Ministry) that had attacked lives and liberties, etc. A moot plea, one would have thought—Campbell thought so; but ultimately unpersuasive.

Still the fragments speak for themselves. Of the defense witnesses represented here one can only admit that while they spoke well enough for *themselves,* the courtroom was not their arena. True, John Adams was a lawyer, but on the witness stand this could only tell against him. He was too easily trapped into defending his own legalistic niceties. Jefferson was perhaps a great writer, certainly a great politician, perhaps a great philosopher (obviously influenced by Mr. Hutcheson), but he was not a good speaker. The defense, even so, probably saw these as preferable witnesses to Washington himself. It is well known that he mumbled and was embarrassed by his artificial, wooden teeth.

The fragments speak for themselves and so they must, for I must rest. I was scarcely born at the time and now am close to the end. I will put this and the fragments into the box. My dear, good Anne will know to open it should I not last until she returns from England. What a time for her aunt to sicken unto death! The world will know of it. Whether it will learn from it—but I philosophize again. A little madiera, then sleep. Why do I even write this, these tired words? A need to leave some mark of my own passing? For I feel I must pass very soon.

I neither fear it nor anticipate it with any great hope of a blessed life to come. I am simply tired. They shall go in the box now. My last task is done. It is not done well, but how often do we meet our own high standards? "Video meliora proboque: deteriora sequor." Then the wine. And sleep.

> Augustin Fox M.A.
> of Trinity College, Dublin;
> and of the Inner Temple
> Barrister-at-Law

FRAGMENTS FROM THE BOX

. . . .

FRAGMENT 1. THE CHARGE AGAINST
COLONEL WASHINGTON

George Washington, it is hereby charged against you that, not having the fear of Almighty God before your eyes, you did wilfully and knowingly engage in treasonous acts against your lawful sovereign His Majesty King George III. Namely, you did compass or imagine the death of the King and the Royal Family by vile plots and connivances; that you did levy war upon the King in his realm by placing yourself at the head of rebel armies; that you did adhere to the King's enemies within his realm, to whit the kings of France and Spain; that you did give aid and comfort to these enemies in his realm and elsewhere; that you have caused the King's justices to be slain; and that by these divers acts you have shown yourself to be a traitor against His Majesty deserving of no mercy but only of the full and terrible penalty of the law.

FRAGMENT 2. THE EVIDENCE OF JUDGE
JONATHAN SEWALL

(*Courtroom*)

THORNTON: State your name and place of residence.

SEWALL: Jonathan Sewall, formerly of the town of Cambridge, in the Massachusetts Bay Colony, now No. 1 Brompton Road, in the City of London.

THORNTON: Thank you. You may proceed, Colonel.

HAMPSHIRE: Mr. Sewall, before moving to London in 1775, you were in turn Solicitor General, Advocate General, and then Attorney General of the Massachusetts Bay Colony, were you not?

SEWALL: I was, sir.

HAMPSHIRE: And now you hold the position of Chief Judge of the Admiralty of Lower Canada?

SEWALL: Of the Vice-Admiralty Bench, sir, of Halifax and Quebec, yes sir.

HAMPSHIRE: You were in Massachusetts during the years preceding the insurrection then, and in Boston during its state of siege?

SEWALL: I was, sir.

HAMPSHIRE: Do you recognize the accused?

SEWALL: I do. He is George Washington, self-styled General and commander of the rebel army.

(*Fenway rises.*)

FENWAY: My Lords, I object. The style of General was conferred on Colonel Washington by the Continental Congress; he was in no way self-styled.

THORNTON: I cannot entertain that objection. This court does not recognise any body calling itself a Continental Congress as having the right to bestow military titles in His Majesty's realms. That privilege belongs to His Majesty the King alone. The prisoner was a colonel of militia and since this is a court martial he can be accorded the courtesy of that title, duly and legally conferred, and none other. Proceed, Colonel Hampshire.

(*Defense sits.*)

HAMPSHIRE: (*Nods and smiles wryly at Fenway.*) On what occasions did you see *Colonel* Washington?

SEWALL: Oh, many, many. He was in and around with his troops the whole time. He was plainly visible.

HAMPSHIRE: And during this time attacks were made upon the King's troops?

SEWALL: Indeed, sir. Of course, sir. We all know that.

HAMPSHIRE: Indeed we do, Mr. Sewall, but we have to have it recorded and established here in court that it was so. How did you know that Colonel Washington styled himself "General"?

SEWALL: Why, sir, we all knew. And when I was assistant to General Gage we received a letter from Washington signed "General." Well, General Gage sent it back, sir, making the Court's point that he could not recognise such a title. And Washington answered that it had been bestowed on him by a higher authority than the King's.

77

(*Consternation in the courtroom*)

HAMPSHIRE: And whose, pray?

SEWALL: That of the people, he said.

(*More consternation*)

HAMPSHIRE: "The people" in this case did not include you and other loyal subjects starving to death in Boston as a result of Washington's designs, presumably.

SEWALL: Scarcely that, sir. There were many thousands trapped there who would rather have seen him with a rope around his neck than a ribbon. And many thousands outside the city who went silently in fear of their lives.

HAMPSHIRE: In other words, Washington was not a true representative of the people from whom he claimed to derive his authority for waging war against the King in his realm.

SEWALL: He represented a faction, sir, only. It was a noisy, brutal, and effective faction, but only a fool would claim it was "the people" of the Colonies.

HAMPSHIRE: How many were in this faction?

SEWALL: I can't say, sir. I can only say they had power and influence beyond their numbers. But I doubt a quarter of the population ever really followed them with conviction.

HAMPSHIRE: If Colonel Washington, then, did not derive his authority from a united people, presumably he would claim that he derived it from the so-called Continental Congress, which in turn derived it from the people?

SEWALL: That would be false. The Continental Congress was an illegal assembly, a contrivance of the Committees of Correspondence, who were also illegal. No one voted for them.

HAMPSHIRE: Did you know the members of the Massachusetts committee?

SEWALL: I did. James Otis, John Hancock, and Sam Adams were the ringleaders.

HAMPSHIRE: What of John Adams?

SEWALL: May I ask a question of the Court?

THORNTON: Certainly, Mr. Sewall.

SEWALL: Must I say anything that might incriminate John Adams? You see, my lord, I know he is in this country and may soon be on trial for his life. And much as I despise his politics, he was and is my friend. Unless the Court finds it absolutely necessary I would be obliged if . . .

THORNTON: Does Counsel wish to press this point?

HAMPSHIRE: No, my lord. We shall proceed, if you will, Mr. Sewall, to the activities of the rebels prior to the insurrection.

SEWALL: Yes, sir. Of course. James Otis and his cabal, the "Caucus Club" were the centre of it. Years before the Declaration of Independence they set up what was virtually an opposition government and took the law into their own hands, exploiting both legitimate and illegitimate grievances to rouse the populace.

HAMPSHIRE: Legitimate grievances, Mr. Sewall? Like what, pray?

SEWALL: The Stamp Act, sir—an act about which we all felt aggrieved. Governors Hutchinson and Bernard worked as hard for its repeal, as did Otis and Sam Adams.

HAMPSHIRE: Their methods, however, were different, I imagine.

SEWALL: Indeed. Governor Hutchinson sent a humble petition to Parliament; Adams intimidated the collectors. Governor Hutchinson would have submitted regretfully had Parliament insisted. Otis and Adams were determined to resist.

HAMPSHIRE: Why?

SEWALL: Because they were hellbent on independency from the start! They had no high principles—John Adams excepted—but they had high ambition and thirst for power. They roused the mob to intimidate the King's officers and to attack their property, family, and lives. They tarred and feathered poor John Malcolm twice! I escaped only by good fortune.

HAMPSHIRE: Escaped? Did you personally experience the results of this activation of the mob?

SEWALL: I did. One day when I was in Boston, some fifty men and boys— "Sons of Liberty," they called themselves, (and Mr. Barré of the House of Commons has much to answer for in coining that wretched phrase). Anyway, these noble defenders of liberty and free speech and the like surrounded my house in Brattle Street in Cambridge, broke all of the windows, threatened the lives of my family, and only made off when my poor terrified wife submitted to their demands for the whole of my wine cellar.

(*Court is horrified.*)

BROOKE: Good God!

HAMPSHIRE: And what brutal and tyrannical things in the name of King and Parliament had you inflicted on these "Sons of Liberty," Mr. Sewall, to arouse their wrath so?

79

SEWALL: Nothing of which I am aware, sir, except that, under various names, I wrote for the local papers articles on good government and vindications of the Governor's character.

HAMPSHIRE: And had the King's officers ever harrassed them or attacked their persons or property?

SEWALL: Never.

HAMPSHIRE: Was Mr. Hancock among those who supported the Sons of Liberty?

SEWALL: Fervently, sir.

HAMPSHIRE: What dealings had you with him in legal matters?

SEWALL: As Advocate General, sir, I was asked to prosecute him on the grounds of information laid against him in the matter of smuggling.

HAMPSHIRE: Was he a well-known smuggler?

SEWALL: Indeed, yes, sir. Confessed and boastful of it.

HAMPSHIRE: How did you proceed?

SEWALL: I refused to proceed.

(*Murmurs in the court*)

SEWALL: There was not sufficient evidence; and the procedure of laying information, which bypassed a grand jury, was not sound.

HAMPSHIRE: Hardly the act of a dupe of the Customs Board.

SEWALL: No, sir. In fact, the Board of Customs complained to the Lords of the Treasury, but they upheld my decision.

HAMPSHIRE: But you did finally prosecute Hancock, did you not?

SEWALL: I was obliged to, sir, by definite evidence being laid against him in regard to his ship, the *Liberty*.

HAMPSHIRE: And did Mr. Hancock, apprised by now of your just dealing, submit himself honestly to the process of law?

SEWALL: No, sir. He and Otis raised the mob again. The Commissioners and myself were endangered and threatened.

HAMPSHIRE: How did you proceed?

SEWALL: Well, sir, I proceeded as I had to. I allowed that we should proceed on the case *in rem* concerning the ship and the cargo aboard under Clause 29 of the Sugar Act, but on the libel *in personam* concerning the smuggling of wine, I refused to proceed on the grounds of insufficient evidence. It was . . .

HAMPSHIRE: Mr. Sewall, there are those here to whom these particular legal matters are a mystery; not least myself. (*Laughter in the court*) Can we say, however, that while allowing a lesser charge you refused to proceed on the graver charge for lack of evidence?

SEWALL: Exactly. The Attorney General of England then ordered me to proceed on the graver charge.

HAMPSHIRE: And you did so.

SEWALL: No, sir. I tendered my resignation to the Governor rather than do so. (*Murmurs in the court*) Eventually, however, the *in personam* libel—the graver charge—was dropped, and I withdrew my resignation.

HAMPSHIRE: Now, Mr. Sewall. You have been painted by the Sons of Liberty as one of the tyrants and villains against whom legitimate rebellion could be waged because of your brutal infringement of their liberties. Hancock and Otis and Adams inveigh against you, vilify and attack and intimidate you. Yet here we see you scrupulously attending to your office to the extent of refusing to prosecute Hancock on the grounds of insufficient evidence—even when it was in your power to do so and when higher authority ordered you to do so. Do you consider Hancock's response a fair response, Mr. Sewall?

SEWALL: Hardly that, sir.

HAMPSHIRE: What was the outcome for yourself, Mr. Sewall, of this sad business?

SEWALL: I had to flee Cambridge, sir, for the protection of Boston and General Gage.

HAMPSHIRE: Who was sent to Boston in response to persistent outrages of the kind you have described?

SEWALL: Indeed, yes, sir. I was one of those who pressed for his presence.

HAMPSHIRE: And your property?

SEWALL: My houses, my farm, my land were all taken and reassigned to others—illegally and without warrant—as were those of other loyal subjects of His Majesty who fled likewise.

HAMPSHIRE: Now, Mr. Sewall. This point is crucial. The defense intends to say that Washington placed himself at the head of an army composed of otherwise loyal Englishmen forced by a tyrannical government to defend themselves against abusive authority. You are a representative of that authority and well qualified to tell this court, in summary, what you make of that defense.

SEWALL: It is sheer hypocrisy, sir. This was a calculated rebellion, led by men who wished to exercise ultimate power. To this end they seized on any excuse presented by legislation that was either precedented and unchallenged, or necessary, or even benign, to assert rights that never existed. They invented tyrannies that never were. They made of men like myself and the Governors scapegoats—men who had dealt them

81

only justice and kindness, despite their open and confessed illegal acts. They roused the populace and formed illegal assemblies; they terrorised and intimidated loyal citizens; they molested the King's troops, and when these defended themselves, they dubbed them murderers.

HAMPSHIRE: Who provoked the first shots in this affair?

SEWALL: The rebels at Lexington, sir. The King's troops were on legitimate business seeking to destroy illegal powder supplies. They were resisted. The rebels will say they were defending liberties, but what liberty is it, sir, to hoard arms in order to fight your legal Sovereign? (*to the judges*) They were not concerned with defense, my lords. Against whom were they defending themselves when they terrorized my wife and children and robbed me of my wine? What tyranny had I, or thousands like me who were forced to flee, exercised over them? No, my lords; they were hell-bent, my lords, hell-bent on power that could only be achieved through independency—through armed rebellion and the murder and intimidation of loyal subjects, forcing us to flee to strange places—to Canada, to England, to New York even! No, my lords, defenders they were not, but tyrants of their own kind ever ready to cry "Liberty" when their designs for power were thwarted.

HAMPSHIRE: Mr. Sewall, if the action of Colonel Washington and his associates was not a justified defense of liberties against tyranny, but a true premeditated rebellion, then from when do you date the commencement of this rebellion?

SEWALL: From the day, sir, that the *Mayflower* set sail from Plymouth!

HAMPSHIRE: Thank you, Mr. Sewall. I have no further questions.

THORNTON: Mr. Fenway. Do you wish to cross-examine?

FENWAY: Yes, indeed, my Lord.

(*Fenway rises.*)

FENWAY: Mr. Sewall, you must understand that it is George Washington on trial here, not the Massachusetts Cabal. I did not intervene during your testimony because it seemed to me that their lordships would see it to be self-evidently irrelevant. I will accept that a faction in Massachusetts comported itself as you describe, but would you tell the court what evidence you have that George Washington was, to quote your words, "hell-bent on independency from the start."

SEWALL: Why, sir, the whole Virginia clique was as bad as the Massachusetts Cabal. Lee, Jefferson, Washington—it was the two cliques between them that led the rest by the nose. There is no distinguishing between them.

FENWAY: I repeat, Mr. Sewall, what *evidence* have you of Washington's rebellious intentions?

SEWALL: His intentions were clear enough. Why—when the Congress was in suspense and a vote for independence was in the balance—what did Washington do? He arrived, sir, in full blue regimentals of the Virginia militia, sir. To impress the recalcitrants.

FENWAY: But that was late in the day, Mr. Sewall. That was after the King's troops had arrived, battles had been fought, and a de facto state of belligerency had come into existence. What evidence is there of longstanding rebellious intent on the part of the prisoner?

SEWALL: Well, sir, how do I know, sir? What goes on in a man's head is his business, sir. I am not privy to that. His intention can be judged by his actions, sir, and they were plain enough.

FENWAY: Not plain enough to establish premeditation, Mr. Sewall. I must insist . . .

HAMPSHIRE: And so must I, my lords. This course of questioning is irrelevant. The witness cannot know what the prisoner secretly intended. He can only report his actions, which he has done.

THORNTON: Really, Mr. Fenway. This line of questioning seems to be going nowhere. Could we not press on?

CAMPBELL: My lord, I feel the Defense may have a point. (*To Fenway*) As I understand it, Mr. Fenway, you are saying that there is no evidence that Colonel Washington intended rebellion before the advent of the troops, and that after that he merely intended to act defensively? I am not agreeing that this is so, but am asking if this is your point.

FENWAY: It is indeed, Sir George.

CAMPBELL: Aye, well. A fine point.

THORNTON: Too fine, perhaps. Mr. Fenway, please press on.

FENWAY: Yes, my lord. Mr. Sewall, you have made much of how you, an impartial administrator of justice, were abused by the radicals in Boston.

SEWALL: Quite so.

FENWAY: And it was only as an impartial servant of justice that you refused to prosecute John Hancock?

SEWALL: Of course.

FENWAY: Would you tell the court your relationship of kinship to John Hancock.

SEWALL: Well—he—he is the husband of my wife's sister. My brother-in-law. But . . .

(*Hampshire rises.*)

HAMPSHIRE: My lords, I object!

(*Thornton uses the gavel.*)

THORNTON: Order, gentlemen! Mr. Fenway, that question is irrelevant, surely?

FENWAY: Well, my lord . . .

CAMPBELL: Oh, I think not, my lord. Credibility of witness is an issue.

HAMPSHIRE: Sir George! The witness is, like yourself, a judge!

CAMPBELL: A guarantee of very little as concerns rectitude, Colonel. Some of the biggest rogues in history have been judges. I am but a judge *pro tempore,* Colonel. No. Credibility is an issue.

SEWALL: But, my lords, he has done nothing but show I was related to Hancock. Good God, sirs, in Massachusetts everyone is related to everyone else!

THORNTON: For pity's sake, gentlemen, let us proceed. Mr. Fenway.

FENWAY: Yes, my lord. Mr. Sewall. Again you have painted yourself as a defender of truth in writing pamphlets and articles in defense of the Governors and the Crown.

SEWALL: Indeed. Yes. I did my best.

FENWAY: And were you not well rewarded by offices and remuneration for your pains?

SEWALL: I rose—achieved advancement—by merit, sir.

FENWAY: Yes. But once advanced you devoted much time and ink to the defense of your employers.

(*Hampshire rises.*)

HAMPSHIRE: My lords . . . !

THORNTON: Yes, Colonel, you object to this attempt to paint Judge Sewall as a paid lackey of the government, and so do I.

CAMPBELL: Credibility, my lord. Credibility.

THORNTON: Mr. Fenway. You have made your point. May we proceed to matters of substance?

FENWAY: My lord, I would if there were any. We have heard much of the activity of the Massachusetts rebels—so-called—but nothing of the prisoner's involvement with them until he took command of the troops outside Boston.

THORNTON: And is that not enough?

FENWAY: No, my lords. No. Not if premeditation is the issue. This witness has proven nothing except that he is a loyal, paid servant of the Crown. He has produced no evidence that Colonel Washington "imagined the death of the King," contrived rebellion, or anything such, merely that he commanded the American armies, which no one is disputing.

HAMPSHIRE: My lords, is there anything else to establish? A man's intentions are not at issue here. His actions are.

CAMPBELL: Well, now, Colonel. If in a case of murder, for example, one is pleading self-defense, then intentions do enter into consideration . . .

THORNTON: Yes, yes, Sir George. But we cannot digress on the law of murder just now. Mr. Fenway, please come to the point.

FENWAY: I have one more point, my lord. Mr. Sewall, you have agreed that Washington took his commission from the Continental Congress. (*Sewall nods.*) Now, you have pictured this body as a cabal of cabals. If it was indeed, sir, a contrivance of the radicals, is it not strange that it was so divided? That it took so long to reach a decision? That it petitioned the King so often?

SEWALL: Yes, yes. There were others than radicals, of course. I said they were a minority. But the congress was illegal, sir. What it argued about was not rebellion—it encouraged that openly. What it argued about, what it was divided about, was independence. And Virginia and Massachusetts pressed and bullied the others to accept *that*.

FENWAY: This was then not just a rebel cabal, but a representative deliberative assembly that argued its way to decisions—including the decision to have George Washington as its Commander-in-chief?

SEWALL: It was an illegal assembly, sir. It countenanced armed rebellion without debate. Its petitions were sops to the loyalists, devices to gain time. And Washington was deep into this, sir, deep into it! He will surely hang for his treachery!

(*Thornton gavels for order.*)

THORNTON: Mr. Sewall. If you please, sir, no more speeches. Your opinion of the prisoner is not at issue; only the facts.

FENWAY: My lord, I submit there *are* no facts of any substance. I will, therefore, not weary the court further with empty accusations. I have no more questions.

THORNTON: Thank you Mr. Fenway. Mr. Sewall, you may step down. Gentlemen, should we proceed to the next witness?

BROOKE: Oh surely not, my lord. It is close to lunchtime already.

THORNTON: In deference to your lordship, court is adjourned until two o'clock.

BROOKE: Perhaps two-thirty . . . ?

THORNTON: Two-thirty . . . (*Gavels*)

FRAGMENT 3. THE EVIDENCE OF GENERAL SIR BENEDICT ARNOLD

(*Courtroom*)

USHER: Call General Sir Benedict Arnold!

SOLDIER: General Sir Benedict Arnold!

(*Arnold enters in full regalia.*)

USHER: Do you swear by Almighty God that the evidence you shall give before this court will be the truth, the whole truth, and nothing but the truth?

ARNOLD: I do.

THORNTON: Please state your name and rank.

ARNOLD: Benedict Arnold, Knight Commander of the Order of St. Michael and St. George, General of his Majesty's forces.

THORNTON: Thank you, Sir Benedict. Proceed, Colonel.

HAMPSHIRE: Sir Benedict. Painful as it may be for you, we must recapitulate something of your involvement with the rebel armies and their commander.

(*Arnold nods assent.*)

HAMPSHIRE: You were, before returning to your allegiance to the Crown, an officer in the rebel army. What rank did you hold?

ARNOLD: That of Brigadier General, sir.

HAMPSHIRE: And in that capacity—with that high rank—you were much involved with the prisoner?

ARNOLD: Yes, sir. He was my Commander-in-chief.

HAMPSHIRE: For the record, then, could you name some of the occasions on which you saw him in command of rebel troops?

ARNOLD: Oh, many, sir. Outside Boston during the siege. At Valley Forge in Pennsylvania where he held the American army together before his brilliant attack on Trenton.

HAMPSHIRE: That will suffice, Sir Benedict. In particular, sir, we would like you to specify for the court whether he, to quote the words of the charge, "conspired with the King's enemies within his realm." That is, allied with the French.

ARNOLD: That he did. Why, when he almost surprised me and I had to flee to the *Vulture* there on Hudson's River, he was on his way to treat with the French. And all the while I was Military Governor of Philadelphia, he was deep into negotiations with them. It was this, sir, in fact, that made me disgusted with the American cause.

HAMPSHIRE: Before we get to that, Sir Benedict, perhaps you would outline the history of your involvement.

ARNOLD: Certainly. Well, sir, before the war started I had been an apothecary. Not much profit in that, y'know, so I turned to one of the most profitable and respectable trades open in America.

HAMPSHIRE: What was that, pray?

ARNOLD: Smuggling, Colonel, smuggling.

(*Murmurs in the court*)

HAMPSHIRE: A respectable trade, Sir Benedict?

ARNOLD: Why, yes. Every other man was a smuggler, and those who weren't profited by it anyway. I made a good living until the British Parliament began to tighten its laws and send out all those revenue cutters and customs officers. That hit us all hard, sir, very hard, and we didn't like it. We didn't like it a bit. And the local Sons of Liberty seized on our dissatisfaction and persuaded us to resist the tyranny of those who wished to invoke the law to our disadvantage.

HAMPSHIRE: You were not, then, much concerned with the arguments about rights and liberty and taxation and sovereignty?

ARNOLD: No, Colonel. If you're an ordinary American, not educated, not of high society, you don't have the time to argue about those things. You're busy making a living. We didn't say, "What are our rights according to the laws of nature?" We said, "My friends have been abused; my pocket's been hurt; I won't stand for it."

HAMPSHIRE: But surely there must have been some qualms about the legality of rebellion? About allegiance to the King?

ARNOLD: Well, Colonel, not much y'know. Ordinary Americans like myself didn't have much to do with England. Not like the gentry with their books and fashions. It was far away. We had no dealings with it. We were Americans. Anyway, we never reckoned we were disloyal to the King. I would never have signed the Declaration of Independence, sir; but like John Dickinson who refused to sign yet joined the continental armies, I decided to fight back when the ministry sent troops over to attack us. We resented that, bitterly, but we didn't so much blame the King for it.

HAMPSHIRE: Then independence was not one of your motives, Sir Benedict?

ARNOLD: No, sir. Not mine. It could well have been others, though. You see, they saw—Ben Franklin and the rest—they saw that America

87

would grow—become a big rich nation. And they wanted to run it themselves—not have it run from Britain. So all these regulations irked them. No expansion westward, all trade to be with Britain, and the like. They wanted rid of these restrictions. But that wasn't in my head, sir. No. Like the prince of smugglers himself, John Hancock, I wanted the cutters off my back and not much else. I was only an apothecary turned smuggler then—nothing to expect from England and much to expect from my clients, my fellow Americans.

HAMPSHIRE: But you nevertheless served with great distinction in the rebel army, moving rapidly to high command, leading attacks in Canada, and defeating Burgoyne at Saratoga. So much we know, Sir Benedict. Now, tell the court about your reasons for deserting the rebel cause.

ARNOLD: Well, Colonel. As I said, I wasn't ever much concerned with the higher issues. I thought the war'd be short, the British army'd go home, and we'd all get back to smuggling again. (*Laughter*) But no. It dragged on. And then independence became the big issue and I'd never liked that much. Then on top of that came the French alliance. Now, sir, to fight amongst ourselves—among Englishmen—was one thing. That was a family quarrel, you might say. But to ally with the Frenchies, sir, the very enemies that English and Americans had stood together to defeat not twenty years before! That was not fighting fair, I thought. I couldn't take that.

HAMPSHIRE: Were you alone?

ARNOLD: Good God, no. Robert Morris, who signed the Declaration, was against it, and Charles Lee, too, but we were drowned out. By this time the fanatics had hold, and when we wanted to treat with the peace commissioners, we were shouted down.

HAMPSHIRE: Was this when you began negotiations with Major André— later murdered at George Washington's order—to return to your true allegiance?

ARNOLD: Yes, sir.

CAMPBELL: Sir Benedict, I wonder if you would indulge my curiosity a moment. You signed your letters to André "Monk," I understand. Why was that?

ARNOLD: Why? Well, Sir George, because I admired General Monk of Cromwell's army who returned to his true allegiance—to Charles II— for the same reasons.

CAMPBELL: What reasons, Sir Benedict?

ARNOLD: Well, Monk saw that the "model army" that arose to defend English liberties against the King had become a worse tyrant than the King himself. The same was true of the American Congress. They were no better than the worst of the Royal Governors. Dishonest, corrupt, riddled with faction, and out for their own privileges—while my men and I suffered at the front. They were not what they appeared to be in their solemn declarations. They were but a bunch of mean, petty-minded speculators. Why, even Washington wrote to me to say that he would do well out of the war since land prices would rise. But Washington was honester than most of 'em. Behaved well enough to me, which is more than I can say about the rest.

CAMPBELL: I see. Thank you, Sir Benedict.

HAMPSHIRE: Nevertheless, Washington did conspire with the French?

ARNOLD: Yes. And for me that was the last straw.

HAMPSHIRE: Was it not also treason?

ARNOLD: The court must decide that.

HAMPSHIRE: But surely, General, you must have thought that it was when you contemplated and rejected the French alliance?

ARNOLD: I suppose so. But it wasn't the treason so much—it was just that it stuck in my throat to join the Frenchies in killing Englishmen.

HAMPSHIRE: Be that as it may, Sir Benedict, others had opinions about treason. What might the Americans have done to you if, after you returned to our side, they had won the war and taken *you* prisoner?

ARNOLD: Hang me for a traitor, I suppose. But they didn't win, sir. We did.

HAMPSHIRE: Quite so, Sir Benedict. Quite so. No more questions, my lords. (*Hampshire sits.*)

THORNTON: Mr. Fenway?

FENWAY: Sir Benedict: Were you not originally a zealous supporter of the American cause?

ARNOLD: At first, sir, yes, I was.

FENWAY: Did you not take the initiative in forcing the Massachusetts assembly to let you attack Fort Ticonderoga—even when it was clear Congress would not approve the attack?

ARNOLD: I did. I don't deny it.

FENWAY: Did you not finance this expedition yourself?

ARNOLD: I did. I expected reimbursement.

FENWAY: Were you not commonly regarded as the best general the Americans had—even by the British?

ARNOLD: I suppose I was. It was not an incorrect judgment, though I'd put Washington a close second.

FENWAY: And despite your zeal, your initiative, your investment and your reputation, were you not repeatedly disappointed by Congress and your colleagues?

ARNOLD: I was disappointed, yes, by the whole bunch except for Washington.

FENWAY: Did they not pass you over for promotion, fail to pay your expenses, deprive you of your seniority?

ARNOLD: Yes, they did . . .

FENWAY: Were you not court-martialed for your conduct as Military Governor of Philadelphia?

ARNOLD: At my own request. To clear my name.

FENWAY: And what was the verdict?

ARNOLD: I was found guilty of two trivial charges, and sentenced to a reprimand.

FENWAY: A reprimand? From whom?

ARNOLD: The Commander-in-Chief. General Washington.

FENWAY: The prisoner.

ARNOLD: Yes.

FENWAY: Thank you. Now, then. Was it not indeed from that date that you decided to plan revenge on them all and change sides?

ARNOLD: Is that what you're getting at? No! Damn it, sir. From before that, sir.

FENWAY: Can you prove that?

ARNOLD: Well. How can I prove it? My wife destroyed my letters when I fled. André burned my notes. But what you're getting at is wrong. My reason was the French Alliance.

FENWAY: The French Alliance? Not bitterness, thwarted ambition, disappointed hopes?

ARNOLD: No. None of these.

FENWAY: If you were against the alliance, Sir Benedict, why did you request a loan from the French Ambassador?

ARNOLD: That? That was a private matter. Congress witheld my money. I had to pay my debts. I didn't care where the money came from. I would've borrowed from the Devil himself.

FENWAY: Of course, one way to avoid debts was to flee to the other side.

ARNOLD: I resent that, sir. That's not why I went. It was the alliance. You're insinuating it was thwarted ambition, but look at the facts: After I had begun negotiations with André my seniority was restored and Washington offered me command of the left wing of the army—the cavalry and light foot. I declined, sir, because of my promise to André and Sir Henry Clinton to take command at West Point.

FENWAY: But only after Clinton had offered you money, a title, and high rank, no?

HAMPSHIRE: My lords, I must object. The witness is not on trial.

THORNTON: Yes, yes, Colonel Hampshire. I think, Mr. Fenway, that your cross-examination does indeed border on harrassment.

CAMPBELL: Well, my lord, he has a point, and should perhaps be allowed to make it.

THORNTON: Yes, yes, Sir George, but in a civil fashion.

CAMPBELL: Well, we could scarcely expect a barrister to do it in a military fashion, my lord.

(*Laughter*)

(*Thornton gavels.*)

THORNTON: Gentlemen, please. Mr. Fenway, do you wish to question the witness further?

FENWAY: One more question, my lord. Sir Benedict, were you subpoenaed to appear at this trial?

ARNOLD: No.

FENWAY: In other words, you appeared voluntarily to give evidence against a man who had defended you and treated you honourably always, and who is now fighting for his life.

(*Hampshire starts to interrupt.*)

FENWAY: Thank you, Sir Benedict, that is all.

FRAGMENT 4: THE EVIDENCE OF MR. JOHN ADAMS

(*Courtroom. John Adams is in the witness box.*)

FENWAY: Mr. Adams, you are by profession a lawyer?

ADAMS: And a farmer, sir, like my father before me.

FENWAY: Lawyer and farmer, then. You are a graduate of Harvard College, and you have been prominent in legal circles in Boston and

Massachusetts. You were a delegate to the Continental Congress, and under the brief independent regime of the American States, you were appointed Chief Justice of Massachusetts?

ADAMS: Yes, sir. I was. It was probably the greatest honour of my life.

(*Murmurs in court*)

FENWAY: You had previously been offered the post of Advocate General of Massachusetts Bay Colony, I believe, by Governor Hutchinson and Attorney General Sewall.

ADAMS: I had, sir, but I declined.

FENWAY: Why was that, Mr. Adams?

ADAMS: By that time, sir, matters had come to a head between those of us who felt the Royal officers were acting oppressively and those who, like Jonathan Sewall, believed them to be acting legitimately. It would have been hypocritical of me to accept a position from those I was bound to oppose on principle.

FENWAY: We shall return to the question of your opposition, Mr. Adams. But first I would like to ask you why, if you were so opposed to the actions of the Crown, you undertook to defend the British soldiers involved in what has become known as the Boston Massacre?

ADAMS: Because, Mr. Fenway, I love justice. The mob and the fanatics would have sacrificed those innocent men for sheer revenge. I could not stand by and see that happen in my beloved commonwealth, which had always cherished the principle of justice and the rule of law.

FENWAY: And would you remind the court of the outcome of that by now notorious trial?

ADAMS: A jury of twelve of my fellow countrymen acquitted the soldiers on the grounds of self-defense. Two were found guilty of manslaughter and subjected to a minor penalty.

(*Murmurs in the court*)

FENWAY: Thank you, Mr. Adams. Now let us proceed to your knowledge of the prisoner. You had, I believe, a direct hand in his elevation to Commander-in-Chief?

ADAMS: Yes, indeed. I proposed him for that position. My cousin, Samuel Adams, was the seconder.

FENWAY: It is charged, Mr. Adams, that his acceptance of that post makes him guilty of the crime of treason—of which, by implication, you must be an accomplice. What do you say to this charge?

THORNTON: I must remind the witness that he need not say anything that might incriminate him. Do you understand that, Mr. Adams?

ADAMS: Yes, my lord. But since I am no more guilty of treason than George Washington, I am not afraid to speak my mind.

THORNTON: Very well. Proceed, Mr. Fenway.

FENWAY: Thank you, my lord. Mr. Adams?

ADAMS: No, sir, it was not treason. George Washington's appointment and his acceptance of command were among many actions taken out of dire and desperate necessity, and in great sorrow. You must understand how we stood at that time. We were proud of our liberties, our rights as inshrined in our charters, our common law, and our traditions of responsible self-government. We were proud also of our ties of loyalty and kinship with Britain, but these ties had been strained. Over the years attack after attack had been made by the ministers upon our liberties, which we had resisted, as was our right through all legal and constitutional means open to us. Since we had no representation in Parliament, we resisted by resolutions, by petitions to the King and Parliament, and by actions in the courts. We were rebuffed at every turn. In moments of anger, sir, some of our people responded with excesses of which none of us wholly approved, although we sympathized with their frustrations. As a result, our port was closed, our manufactures ruined, troops were sent against us. In short, we were treated like naughty children rather than responsible adults who had for generations governed their own affairs. We are a proud people, Mr. Fenway, and we would not submit. In the end, unhappily, as you know, fighting broke out, our people were killed, and we rose in arms to defend ourselves. Not to sever ourselves from Britain, but simply to say to the ministers: We will not be enslaved without a struggle. By the time we met in Philadelphia for the second time, the ministry was sending a fleet and an army of foreign mercenaries against us. We were at war. We had no choice but to appoint a commander, and I proposed George Washington. It is not treason, sir, to save one's life and liberty from attack. If I am attacked by the law, I defend myself in the courts, and none call it treason. If I am attacked with a gun, I can only defend myself with a gun, and what, sir, makes that into treason?

(*Murmurs in the court*)

FENWAY: Thank you, Mr. Adams. Mr. Sewall has said, however, that there was a faction "hell-bent on independency from the start." Were you of that faction? Or is Mr. Sewall not telling the truth?

ADAMS: Jonathan Sewall never told a lie in his life, sir! He has a different view of things from mine—but that is to be expected. In answer to your question: there was a faction, very small, to whom the idea of independency was sweet. I was not one of them, until it was too late to contemplate anything else. But you must remember, sir, that we were a very political people. We had our conservatives, our moderates, our radicals, our zealots, and of course our mob. No Londoner needs to be lectured on the nature of mobs. But one cannot characterize the whole of a people by its extremes. I would certainly not represent all the English as raving radicals or mobsters because there are some radicals and there is a mob.

(*Murmurs of assent in court*)

FENWAY: But in the end, Mr. Adams, the break did come. You did declare for independence—and you and Washington were firm for it. It has been argued here that this was your aim all along. Is this so?

ADAMS: No, sir. Again we were forced into that position. Our petitions had been ignored. And Parliament and the King declared us to be "in open rebellion." We were to be treated as enemies, our ships as enemy prizes. Armies were to be sent to subdue us. What choice had we, sir? It was they who declared us independent long before we so declared ourselves.

(*Murmurs*)

FENWAY: Is not a long history of disobedience of the King's laws—particularly on taxation—evidence of premeditation and intent to rebel?

ADAMS: No, sir. The issue is not one of obedience by one party to another, but the obedience of both to the Constitution, and the established practices, written and unwritten, by which the colonies and the mother country had lived in harmony. I would say, sir, that it is fairer to say that the King and Parliament disobeyed the Constitution, than that we disobeyed the King and Parliament. They, sir, were the rebels—not we.

(*Murmurs*)

ADAMS: No one considers the Glorious Revolution of 1688 treasonable, and then the British threw out a Monarch who abused their rights. The Americans today did no more than their English cousins had done. They defended the Constitution against attack.

FENWAY: But the issue will be raised, Mr. Adams: are subjects ever justified in making such judgments for themselves—albeit they sometimes succeed by force in doing so?

ADAMS: I would say they are not so justified if they act lightly, without just cause, or for personal gain. This was not true of the Americans. Only after great deliberation, many petitions, and much suffering did they take the irrevocable step; and when they did so, it was solely to protect the principles of liberty and self-government at the heart of the Constitution—principles that are the birthright of all Englishmen.

(*Applause*)

(*Thornton gavels.*)

FENWAY: Thank you, Mr. Adams. I have no more questions.

(*Hampshire rises.*)

HAMPSHIRE: Mr. Adams. Might I say, however much I might disagree with your arguments, I admire greatly the clarity and skill with which they were presented. I think we are all grateful that the defense has been so ably served.

ADAMS: Thank you, sir.

HAMPSHIRE: I have listened, not unmoved, to your statements of the high principles on which the rebels acted. If indeed this were the case, then I think there is not a man here who would not accord some measure of sympathy to you and your fellow Americans in your distress and your struggle for the preservation of your liberties. Your convincing precision in these matters has laid the issue squarely before us, to wit: When the King or his ministers make vicious and tyrannical incursions into the liberties of the people—liberties guaranteed by the Constitution—then the people can, nay, must resist. Is that not so?

ADAMS: Yes, sir. That is what I argued.

HAMPSHIRE: And argued brilliantly, Mr. Adams. So let us examine some of these unconstitutional incursions into your liberties, shall we? Perhaps, Mr. Adams, you could, with your precise, legal mind, enlighten the court on that burning issue that sent your countrymen flying for their muskets—the issue of internal versus external taxation. For was that not one of the most tyrannical and most resisted of the evil measures? Tell us, sir, why was internal taxation so much worse than external, and what, pray, was the difference? Remember, sir, we are not all lawyers, just plain men of common sense.

ADAMS: The distinction was an important one, sir. We had always accepted the right of Parliament to tax us *externally,* that is to lay taxes on goods coming from abroad and the like; but this had to be distinguished from their right to tax us *internally,* that is, to raise revenue directly from us by taxes on, for example, our legal documents. We had always understood it to be our right, not Parliament's, to decide on direct, internal taxation.

HAMPSHIRE: Now, Mr. Adams. Forgive me if I am confused. To me, sir, a tax is a tax. It takes money from my pocket. Now, sir, on your principle, if the Government had put huge taxes on imported goods, that would have been very well, but even a *minuscule* tax on documents would be an occasion for rebellion? Forgive me if I find this odd.

ADAMS: You may find it odd, sir, we did not. It was a matter of principle . . .

HAMPSHIRE: Ah, yes, Mr. Adams, principle, Mr. Adams. I have yet to see, though, quite what the principle is.

ADAMS: Sir: If you put a tax on goods, I may or may not buy them, thus avoiding the tax if I choose. If you tax me directly I cannot avoid paying.

HAMPSHIRE: But if the external tax is on necessities, Mr. Adams, am I not equally forced to pay it? And what of the post office that you accepted? Are not charges for postal stamps a tax?

ADAMS: No, sir, they are a *quantum meruit;* a payment for service rendered.

HAMPSHIRE: But in effect, Mr. Adams, the distinction is a fine one, and the external taxes could be more burdensome, in fact, than the rather trivial internal ones?

ADAMS: They could be, yes . . .

HAMPSHIRE: So it was, at its extremities, something of a legal quibble, eh, Mr. Adams?

ADAMS: Well, sir, it was much argued and the fine points . . .

HAMPSHIRE: Quibbled over, Mr. Adams. Tell me, sir, how many of the King's subjects died in this war?

ADAMS: I think between twenty and thirty thousand, Colonel.

HAMPSHIRE: And for a quibble, Mr. Adams—for a quibble? Let us go on. When Lord Townshend accepted the quibble, sir, when he proposed only external taxes, then, sir, the patient defenders of liberty switched horses, did they not? Could you explain to us, again, Mr. Adams, why you did not accept Lord Townshend's capitulation on this great issue of principle?

ADAMS: Because, sir, Lord Townshend made the external taxes answer to all the purposes of internal taxes.

HAMPSHIRE: Ah, the cunning of the man! Caught you out, did he? Well, well, well.

(Laughter)

HAMPSHIRE: And how did he do this, pray, Mr. Adams?

ADAMS: By making taxes that appeared to be in regulation of trade in fact answer to the purpose of taxes for raising revenue. I had always . . .

HAMPSHIRE: Hold a moment, sir! Did I not detect yet another high principle? What was it—regulation of trade versus raising of revenue? The former just and the latter vicious and tyrannical? Is that right, Mr. Adams? And how does it relate to the previous quibble—I mean distinction, sir?

ADAMS: The distinction is common enough in English law, sir. It is not an American invention.

HAMPSHIRE: But it was seized upon, was it not? When Townshend's acts were repealed and you were satisfied on that count, you had to turn to this other quibble lest the momentum of your movement for independence—your attempts to work up the indignation of the colonies—was lost, eh, Mr. Adams?

ADAMS: No, sir. It was a genuine issue of principle.

HAMPSHIRE: Of principle, Mr. Adams! Yes, of principle! A principle so obscure that even your precise legal mind cannot make it clear to us. How many deaths, Mr. Adams, in this conflict?

ADAMS: I said, sir, about 30,000, I think.

HAMPSHIRE: All went to their deaths, Mr. Adams, because of principles so obscure we cannot make sense of them? When His Majesty's Government generously allows you the first point you scuttle to a second in desperation. Is this not evidence that you had decided to rebel and were deliberately searching for excuses?

ADAMS: There were other causes, sir, many other causes.

HAMPSHIRE: Mr. Adams, there had better have been. Was one of these great causes the wicked, tyrannical, and vicious tax on legal documents known as the Stamp Act?

ADAMS: It was.

HAMPSHIRE: What was the purpose of the Stamp Act?

ADAMS: To raise revenue.

HAMPSHIRE: Ah, yes, and therefore iniquitous under Quibble Number Two. What was this revenue for?

ADAMS: Ostensibly to pay for the expenses of the French War.

HAMPSHIRE: Ostensibly? Were there not such expenses?

ADAMS: Yes, but we had contributed, and if more was needed it should have been left to our assemblies to vote it.

HAMPSHIRE: And it was iniquitous of Parliament to try to raise some trivial sum through stamps?

ADAMS: We judged it so.

HAMPSHIRE: All of you, Mr. Adams?

ADAMS: What do you mean, sir?

HAMPSHIRE: Did not Dr. Franklin attempt to obtain a position as distributor of stamps for his friend Mr. Hughes? Was this testimony to the act's iniquity? And did not "General" Lee, now awaiting his own trial, try to obtain such a post?

ADAMS: I cannot be responsible for the misjudgment of my friends. These things were not always clearly appreciated.

HAMPSHIRE: Not clearly appreciated by the great defenders of constitutional liberty, Mr. Adams? Not clearly appreciated? And on the basis of this lack of clarity, 30,000 men went to their miserable deaths?

ADAMS: There were other causes.

HAMPSHIRE: Indeed there would have to have been, Mr. Adams. The great cause of the tax on tea, perhaps. Was that an internal versus external trade problem or a revenue versus regulation quibble, Mr. Adams?

ADAMS: It was the general principle of taxation . . .

HAMPSHIRE: Ah, the general principle . . . But, Mr. Adams, was it not the case that this wicked and tyrannical parliament and this unconstitutional monarch decided on a plan to produce for their tea-loving subjects cheaper tea?

ADAMS: The tea was cheaper, yes.

HAMPSHIRE: And did not the people in the colonies cheerfully pay the tax?

ADAMS: Most paid.

HAMPSHIRE: Until the famous Boston Tea Party when several of your fellow defenders of liberty and rights dumped this providentially cheap beverage into the sea. Did not your representative here in London, Dr. Franklin, express horror at the extremity of the act? Did he not offer to pay for the tea from his own fortune?

ADAMS: I cannot say.

HAMPSHIRE: Well, I can, sir. And this tyrant, sir, this wicked usurper of rights, this infamous King, asked only one question of his minister when he heard of Boston's rebellious act—"Will my people in Boston," he asked, "be able to get their tea?"

(*Murmurs*)

ADAMS: His response then was strange, for he occupied the town and took away our liberties.

HAMPSHIRE: And what else was any chief magistrate—as you would say—of any commonwealth to do when his authority was flouted on such flimsy grounds by those who clearly intended, given cause or no, to defy his laws and destroy the property of his subjects? Perhaps your friend Mr. Hancock was afraid that his profitable smuggling might be undermined by such generosity from the King and Parliament.

ADAMS: That was never an issue with me, or, more to the point, with General Washington.

HAMPSHIRE: Then what was, Mr. Adams? What was? So far we have isolated no issues that do not, on examination, slip from our grasp like wet soap. What issues? Taxes? Tea? These are mere excuses, sir, and when robbed of one you seize another. What issues? Liberty? Rights?

These are empty words, sir, empty words used to rouse passion in simple minds by men unscrupulous in their lust for power. If these are the best you can produce in the way of causes and justifications for rebellion against the Crown, Mr. Adams, then your sanctimonious claims to be a defender of constitutional liberties are patently false. I have no more to ask.

THORNTON: In that case . . .

BROOKE: My lord . . . ?

THORNTON: Yes of course, my lord. We shall reconvene after lunch. (*Gavels*)

FRAGMENT 5. THE EVIDENCE OF MR. THOMAS JEFFERSON

(*Courtroom. Jefferson is on the stand.*)

FENWAY: Would you state your name and place of residence?

JEFFERSON: Thomas Jefferson of Monticello in the Commonwealth of Virginia.

FENWAY: Mr. Jefferson, you of all people are familiar with the exact events that led up to the signing of the Declaration of Independence, and the painful decision to take up arms against the King's troops. It has been mentioned here that these constituted premeditated acts of treason, and that the prisoner, in placing himself at the head of the American forces, is guilty of treason. Can you answer that charge?

JEFFERSON: Treason was never our intention, sir.

FENWAY: It is however argued that it *was* your intention, that you were "hell-bent on independency." Can you elaborate on your denial?

JEFFERSON: Well, sir. There was no question of premeditated rebellion. It was a cumulation of events. Nothing had been further from our minds than independence. Dr. Franklin testified as much before the House of Commons in 1766, when he said he had never heard a word for independence from any person drunk or sober. There were grievances sir. There was opposition to acts of Parliament, yes; and there were some foolish actions by the mob. But independence, never. Redress of grievances was all that was sought and that by nonviolent acts like boycotts—and no law compelled us to buy British goods—and by petitions—always loyal, always conciliatory.

FENWAY: Could you give examples of the latter?

JEFFERSON: Certainly. The Congress of 1765 declared its sentiments for the perpetual continuance of the tie; the most radical Whigs endorsed this. Even James Otis, protesting against the taxation policy of 1768, deemed independence the greatest misfortune. Massachusetts is painted as the most radical, but in 1774 its House of Representatives, led by Sam Adams, instructed its members to work for unity and harmony. The first Continental Congress of that year sent a loyal address and petition for redress of grievances fully accepting Royal authority and questioning only acts of Parliament.

FENWAY: But fighting started in '75, and it has been held that you were plotting independence and training troops to this end.

JEFFERSON: No, sir. These troops were only the regular militia. Others, like the Minutemen, were merely citizens alarmed at the arrival of 2,000 troops in Boston in '68. They only armed in anticipation of attacks upon themselves.

FENWAY: Was George Washington ever for independence at this time?

JEFFERSON: Never. I remember talking to a friend of Washington's who met him as he was on his way to Congress in '75. This friend said to him: "You are leading the people to civil war and independence." Washington replied that if ever he was known to have joined himself to such an effort, he could be set down for everything wicked. Now this was in May. Lexington had been in April. And he would never let his troops refer to the British as the "King's troops", always "the Ministry's troops"—at first, I mean.

HAMPSHIRE: My lords, this evidence of the prisoner's motives is mere hearsay.

THORNTON: I must agree, Colonel Hampshire.

CAMPBELL: Well, now, milord. It is consistent with other things we have heard about the accused. We should perhaps note it.

THORNTON: Yes, yes—note it and pass on, I think, without hearsay.

FENWAY: Yes, milord. Mr. Jefferson: It will be maintained that even while you were proferring olive branches you were arming and attacking the King's troops.

JEFFERSON: We had no recourse but to arm in self-defense, and we never attacked but were attacked ourselves. Even as we were forced to arm, we expressed an abhorrence of separation. New York, New Hampshire, New Jersey, Delaware, and Maryland all instructed their delegates to have nothing to do with independence. As to arms, we had to convince Parliament of our firmness of purpose. That was all.

FENWAY: What further attempts were made at reconciliation?

JEFFERSON: Several, but chiefly Mr. Dickinson's "Olive Branch" petition. "Right our wrongs, withdraw your armies, remove your tyrannical officials," it said, "and you will have no more loyal subjects than ourselves. But if these things are not done, we must fight rather than be enslaved."

(*Murmurs in the court*)

FENWAY: And what was the King and Parliament's response to this olive branch?

JEFFERSON: The petition was disregarded. On the day he was to have received it—and he refused—His Majesty denounced us as traitors in Parliament and declared us rebels who wanted, in his words, "to establish an independent empire."

FENWAY: What was the reaction of Congress?

JEFFERSON: Shock and horror. Even those most violently opposed to independence, sir, came to see that their hands were being forced. King and Parliament had declared them rebels even as they pronounced their loyalty. The King, with 12,000 Germans, meant to punish them: they had no means of redress; they had to fight.

FENWAY: Was the decision on independence immediate and unanimous?

JEFFERSON: No. It was still much debated. But finally it was unanimous.

FENWAY: As was the decision to appoint George Washington Commander-in-Chief.

JEFFERSON: Yes, sir.

FENWAY: In summary, then, Mr. Jefferson, there was no treasonable intent on the part of the prisoner, or yourself, or any other Americans, until you were forced to arms in self-defense against punitive measures by King and Parliament.

JEFFERSON: That is exactly the case, sir.

FENWAY: My Lords, I have no more questions to ask Mr. Jefferson.

(*Hampshire rises.*)

HAMPSHIRE: My Lords, I am not going to concern myself with the question of the honesty of these petitions, protestations of loyalty and the like. I will let that pass. Whatever hesitancy it might, and should have, shown, the rebel congress finally declared for independence and produced this remarkable paper (*He waves a document*) this so-called "Declaration of Independence" to justify its action to the world. I understand, Mr. Jefferson, that this is largely your handiwork?

JEFFERSON: I drafted it, sir. It was amended by Congress.

HAMPSHIRE: Then I shall concentrate on this, for here is the distilled essence of the American case, the basis for insisting that Washington is not a traitor but a loyal subject forced by a wicked King to defend his liberty. I will not bother, milords, with the rather wordy Preamble. I find it largely unintelligible, the opinions of modern Americans on government being as bizarre as those of their ancestors on witchcraft . . .

CAMPBELL: No more bizarre than the opinions of his late Majesty King James, Colonel. If, Colonel Hampshire, you do not wish to deal with this Preamble, then you will allow me to ask the witness a question or two regarding it.

HAMPSHIRE: Certainly, milord.

(*Thornton nods assent.*)

CAMPBELL: Mr. Jefferson, in your eloquently written preamble you have advanced a theory of government that I find decidedly odd. You say that men have inalienable rights to life, liberty, and the pursuit of happiness; that governments are instituted to this end; and that if governments fail to preserve these rights they can be abolished. Now, sir, is that your intent?

JEFFERSON: It is, Sir George.

CAMPBELL: Surely what you mean is that men have the right to *enjoy* liberty, *enjoy* life, and *enjoy* happiness. Now, any one man's enjoyment of these ends is likely to interfere with the liberty of another, is it not?

JEFFERSON: It could, sir.

CAMPBELL: Then governments exist, Mr. Jefferson, precisely to abridge one man's rights so that they may not so interfere. The essence of government, Mr. Jefferson, is then the abridgment of liberty, and it cannot be faulted for abridgment of liberty per se. I do not wish to make a big issue of it. Lord Kames would have held—

THORNTON: Yes, yes, Sir George, but perhaps we should let prosecution continue?

(*Hampshire rises.*)

HAMPSHIRE: Thank you. My Lords, I will concentrate on the so-called complaints against His Majesty. And let the court take careful note; for here is the solemn and declared case for the awful decision, here is the overwhelming evidence for the right of the rebel armies under George Washington to wage war on the King's troops and ally with the King's enemies.

CAMPBELL: And on this issue, too, milords, I have a question for Mr. Jefferson. With your Lordships' permission . . .

THORNTON: Yes, of course, Sir George.

CAMPBELL: I find it remarkable, Mr. Jefferson, that while the arguments of your Congress had been all against Parliament with protestations of loyalty to the King, in your Declaration here, Parliament is never mentioned and the King is sorely abused. If the grievances were indeed against Parliament, then why was it not here indicted?

JEFFERSON: Congress did not agree that Parliament had any authority over it, so only the matter of dissolving allegiance to the King was involved.

CAMPBELL: Then it seems to me, Mr. Jefferson, that you were more interested in making history than in writing it. Please proceed, Colonel Hampshire.

HAMPSHIRE: Let us turn to the complaint that the King: (*He reads from the Declaration.*) "called together legislative bodies at places unusual, uncomfortable, and distant from the repository of their public records, for the sole purpose of fatiguing them into complaisance with his measures." This was a Massachusetts complaint, was it not?

JEFFERSON: Primarily, yes.

HAMPSHIRE: Massachusetts had the most complaints, did it not?

JEFFERSON: At least it complained the most, yes.

(*Laughter*)

HAMPSHIRE: Where was the unusual place in question?

JEFFERSON: In 1768 the Assembly was moved from Boston to Cambridge.

HAMPSHIRE: And was this not because the Assembly itself objected to meeting in Boston with General Gage's troops there, Mr. Jefferson?

JEFFERSON: They had objected to the presence of the troops, yes.

HAMPSHIRE: And the move to Cambridge involved what distance?

JEFFERSON: About four miles.

HAMPSHIRE: Four miles, yes. And was, of course, utterly without precedent.

JEFFERSON: It had happened once before when there was smallpox in Boston.

HAMPSHIRE: Quite so. And what was the uncomfortable place where they were forced to meet, Mr. Jefferson?

JEFFERSON: The meeting hall of Harvard College.

HAMPSHIRE: Really? Most uncomfortable. . . . On the matter of fatigue, Mr. Jefferson, how often was the Assembly called?

JEFFERSON: I believe it was every day.

HAMPSHIRE: Then the Governor had to drive out from Boston every day.

JEFFERSON: I suppose so.

HAMPSHIRE: Mr. Jefferson, are you aware that once the Governor arrived the Assembly promptly adjourned, forcing him to drive back again?

(*Laughter*)

HAMPSHIRE: The only person, Mr. Jefferson, who would seem to have been unduly fatigued by this arrangement was the unfortunate Governor.

(*More laughter*)

HAMPSHIRE: Do you not consider rebellious claims to independence, war, ravage, destruction, and the deaths of thousands of Englishmen to be a serious and terrible thing, Mr. Jefferson?

(*Laughter dies.*)

JEFFERSON: Naturally. Of course.

HAMPSHIRE: And yet you produce this farce, this piece of tomfoolery, as justification for so terrible an action?

JEFFERSON: It was but a part, and in any case the complaints were not in themselves a justification for rebellion.

HAMPSHIRE: Then what were they, pray?

JEFFERSON: They were a proof that the King was deliberately trying to subjugate and enslave us. No one denied his right to legislate, to refuse his assent to legislation, or anything else; he had all these rights, but he had not the right to establish over us an absolute tyranny, to place us under absolute despotism.

HAMPSHIRE: Then let us examine this despotism, this absolute tyranny, against which, should it exist, you would rightfully complain . . . Let us take . . . (*He scans the document.*) these charges: "That the King has refused his assent to laws. That he has refused to pass laws and refused to attend to them." Now, Mr. Jefferson, you have said that you did not question the King's rights in these matters. And in what sense can you blame this King for policies that had been enacted towards the Colonies by all previous Kings and were enshrined in their charters?

JEFFERSON: It was not the rights as such, it was the abuse of those rights. This King struck down more laws of more kinds than his predecessors.

HAMPSHIRE: And what subtle mathematics of morality decided the number of such acts that was tyrannical and justification for rebellion? Ten acts a year perhaps was tolerable, Mr. Jefferson, but twenty justified taking up arms? What number?

JEFFERSON: It was not simply the number, it was the intent.

HAMPSHIRE: Interesting. When we cannot fix on quantity we rush to a quality. I admire the American legal mind. It was the intent, Mr. Jefferson. And who judged the King's intentions?

JEFFERSON: His intention was clear from his repeated refusals of assent and suspensions. His intent was despotism.

HAMPSHIRE: And as a result of the King's despotism and before armed hostilities began, how many Americans were hanged at the King's orders?

JEFFERSON: None that I know of, but . . .

HAMPSHIRE: And how many languished in prison as a result of the King's arbitrary acts?

JEFFERSON: None, but . . .

HAMPSHIRE: And how many lost their property without due cause and fair trial?

JEFFERSON: Again none, but . . .

HAMPSHIRE: And how many newspapers were closed, books burned, authors tortured?

JEFFERSON: None, but . . .

HAMPSHIRE: But what, Mr. Jefferson? Where is your tyranny, your despotism, except in your own obscure reckonings, sir—your metaphysical mathematics, sir, which tell you and your conspiratorial friends in some mysterious way best known to yourselves that the King has refused his assent to one act too many this year so that bloody rebellion against him is justified?

JEFFERSON: There was a cumulation of acts of tyranny that—

HAMPSHIRE: Indeed there was, Mr. Jefferson. Indeed. A cumulation. Let us look at some other examples of this vicious tyrant's deeds. Let us examine the charge that he has "affected to render the military independent of and superior to the civil power," referring to General Gage's appointment as Governor of Massachusetts, no doubt?

JEFFERSON: Yes.

HAMPSHIRE: Mr. Jefferson, when during the course of hostilities, you withdrew as civil Governor of Virginia, in favour of whom did you withdraw?

JEFFERSON: General Nelson.

HAMPSHIRE: Indeed. Then by what hypocrisy do you condemn in the King an action that you yourself took on another occasion?

JEFFERSON: It was a different case.

HAMPSHIRE: Indeed, yes. In the King's case tyranny, in yours, expediency. Now let us examine the charge that the King "imposed taxes without our consent." The slogan your compatriot Patrick Henry made so popular was "No taxation without representation," I believe. Would you tell the court, Mr. Jefferson, whether all Americans were represented in the colonial assemblies that taxed them?

JEFFERSON: Not all—directly.

HAMPSHIRE: Not directly?

JEFFERSON: No. But those who were not qualified to be were virtually represented by the others; their landlords, for example, their creditors, merchants.

HAMPSHIRE: *Virtually* represented. *Virtually* represented? And how many Englishmen are *directly* represented in their own Parliament?

JEFFERSON: Not all, again.

HAMPSHIRE: But perhaps, here, too, those who are not are *virtually* represented?

JEFFERSON: It could be argued, has indeed often been so argued. I did not invent the distinction, sir. It is common in English political thinking.

HAMPSHIRE: Be that as it may, Mr. Jefferson, we are concerned here with your use of it. So, tell me: Were not the Americans, in that case, *virtually* represented in Parliament through their landlords, creditors, merchants in England?

JEFFERSON: There was a difference. America is 3,000 miles away. For a man to be in touch with his landlord in his own town and have him as a representative in an assembly is one thing. To have a creditor 3,000 miles away is another.

HAMPSHIRE: A fine point, Mr. Jefferson. Nicely argued. On such fine points, on such delicate quibbles as "virtual" representations and the number of acts to which His Majesty can refuse assent without being a tyrant, does the justification for bloody rebellion turn, it seems. Let us look then further at the iniquitous tyrannies of the King. "For transporting us beyond the seas to be tried for pretended offenses." Mr. Jefferson, how many people did the King so transport?

JEFFERSON: None, I think.

HAMPSHIRE: I think so too, Mr. Jefferson. Such tyranny! And an act passed, not by His Majesty, but by King Henry VIII! And, milords, need I detain the court on the most specious section of a specious document: the complaint that the King sent troops to suppress rebellion? Is it an argument *for* rebellion that the King sent troops to suppress one that undeniably already existed? And finally, Mr. Jefferson, your complaint about the Quebec Act—you objected to the establishment of the Catholic Church there? As a result of a petition from the people of Quebec to His Majesty?

JEFFERSON: We did. And the extension of Quebec's boundaries at the expense of our own.

HAMPSHIRE: Really, Mr. Jefferson. You complain that His Majesty won't listen to your petitions, but complain also that he does listen to Quebec's. You cannot have it both ways, sir. But presumably you believe Catholics should have as few rights as Negroes.

JEFFERSON: The analogy is false.

HAMPSHIRE: But the hypocrisy is real, sir. May I remind you of Dr. Johnson's words that the yelps for liberty seem to come loudest from the drivers of slaves?

FENWAY: Milords, that is irrelevant.

THORNTON: Yes, yes. Proceed, Colonel Hampshire.

HAMPSHIRE: I am forced to conclude, my lords, that there is no substance or honesty in this specious document. Mr. Jefferson talks much of liberty and rights, but when asked to defend his specific so-called charges against the King, he shows them to be fallacious and hypocritical and even ludicrous . . . They relate either to things that the King did that were in his power to do, that his predecessors had done, or that the colonists themselves acknowledged his right to do. That some colonists—and nowhere near the majority—did not like what the King did is neither here nor there. A child may not like what its parent does, but this is not justification for murdering the parent. Even if the list of charges could in any way be sustained, it would still not constitute cause for rebellion. The only possible conclusion is that the rebellion the prisoner led was premeditated and intended, as witnesses have shown, and that this treacherous document is no more than a string of post facto justifications not worth the paper it is written on. (*He sits.*)

THORNTON: Mr. Jefferson, you may step down. Court is adjourned until tomorrow morning.

FRAGMENT 6. THE VERDICT OF THE COURT

(*Thornton gavels for order.*)

THORNTON: The court has reached its verdict. It has listened to much argument and has been impressed by both sides. It has been concerned that the Defense should make as elaborate a case as it wished, since it does not regard a man's life—particularly the life of such a man as Colonel Washington—as a thing lightly to be disposed of. It has heard the undeniable facts of his command of rebel armies, his attacks on the King's troops, and his alliance with the King's enemies. These are not in dispute. It has heard the Defense plea that, nevertheless, these actions did not constitute treason since they were essentially defensive and unpremeditated and resulted from the wickedness of the King and his ministers rather than the rebellious intentions of the colonists. However, whatever merit they may have as political or philosophical arguments, after much deliberation, the Court is forced to conclude that there is little merit in these pleadings as they affect the issue of Washington's treason. For essentially they say that his objective treason should be forgiven because his reasons were noble and his grievances sore. Such a doctrine would lead to absolute anarchy, which no state could countenance. It is all too easy, having committed treason, then to plead that it was for noble reasons. Indeed, there can scarcely have been a rebel who did not think he had just and honest cause for his rebellion. It must be obvious to Defense that such a doctrine is untenable. The law of treason takes no account of the reasons for action. It says only that the accused should have understood the consequences of his action. There is no question that Washington committed open treason. The facts are not in dispute, and he cannot, having lost his rebellion, plead that he meant well and was justified. The Court therefore has no choice but to find him guilty of that offense and to pass sentence upon him. Prisoner will rise.

(*Washington stands.*)

THORNTON: Have you anything to say before the sentence of this court is passed upon you?

FRAGMENT 7: STATEMENT OF COLONEL WASHINGTON

My Lords, I thank you for the opportunity to speak. I must first state again what I believe to be the true legal and moral position: That I cannot be guilty of treason because I am a prisoner of war, having been the commander of the army of an independent state at war with Great Britain. On the first day of this trial, the United States of America were deemed not to exist because the Americans had lost the war. But, my Lords, that cannot be true. Had England lost the war she would not therefore have ceased to exist; even if she had been conquered, she would have been a conquered nation. The United States of America exist because their people solemnly declared them to exist; they cannot be obliterated simply because they lost a war. America is now a conquered nation, but it will not always remain so; and when it regains—not its nationhood, but its independence, then the charter for its existence will be that very Declaration that the court here dismissed. This being so, my Lords, I state again that I am the commander-in-chief of the armies of an independent state and therefore not guilty of treason against His Majesty, but only of opposing his troops honourably in the field of battle.

But, my Lords, even the founding of new nations is not the real issue here. While I am not surprised by this verdict, nevertheless you see before you a man who is surprised. I, too, have listened carefully to the arguments of both sides here, and I have come to the conclusion that the law is a fickle thing. I have been raised to revere the law. Yet, as we all know, the judgment of treason would not have been passed upon me and my compatriots had we won. So it seems, astoundingly, that under the law, might is indeed right. Because we lost, we are wrong, we are traitors. Had we won, we would have been right, we would have been saviours. In the face of this logic, it is impossible not to ask whether there is not a higher law than that of the land, a law that does not change, a law to which all men of reason must listen. I accept the judgment of this court, but I accept also that I was led, with my countrymen, by a law that is superior to that of this court, and I cannot escape the conclusion that that law is the one that those who follow after me must listen to. Yesterday, we had the honour of hearing three gentlemen of high conscience who had searched their minds and decided they could not participate in the war against America. Had they not been men of position and influence, had they been simple soldiers, they would not have had the luxury of exercising that conscience. They would have been told that His Majesty's government knew what was right, that the law is clear that a man shall serve his king, and that the law must be right. That is a grave danger for them, for as we have seen, had the British forces failed to win, they would have been judged wrong. This may seem to you, gentlemen, very simpleminded, but to me it is a revelation. If the law is dependent on victory and defeat, then there must be a higher law, a law of humanity, that is not so changeable and to which even victorious nations must bow. For I fear, gentlemen, that even if we had won this war and established yet another new nation, we would certainly have repeated all the mistakes of the old ones: we would have persecuted our own dissenters; tyrannized our own colonies; conducted our own wars of arrogant domination. To this end we would have achieved no step forward. What we must—all of us—look forward to, is a time when it is held that a man cannot rebel against mankind: against human rights and human dignity.

How this can be achieved, I do not know. Men within nations achieve it by meeting in conclave and mutually agreeing to abide by laws they themselves make. Perhaps the time will come when nations themselves will assemble and agree similarly. I do not know. But unless that can be achieved, then all our struggle, and the struggle of those brave Englishmen who supported us, will have been for nothing.

My Lords, I was always told that travelling to London would "broaden my outlook." It is true. It did not quite happen the way I intended, but I am a man with a vision far more exciting now than when I left Yorktown. I thank you for that; the vision is worth dying for, but I hope with all my heart that it does not die with me.

FRAGMENT 8. THE SENTENCE OF THE COURT

George Washington, you have been found guilty of the heinous crime of treason against His Majesty the King. The sentence of this court is that you be taken from here to a place of lawful imprisonment from where at an appointed time you are to be drawn on a hurdle to a place of execution where you are to be hanged by the neck but not until you are dead; for while you are still living your body is to be taken down, your bowels torn out and burned before your face, your head then cut off, and your body divided into four quarters, and your head and quarters to be then at the King's disposal. And may the Almighty God have mercy on your soul.

Three

Children

Of the

Revolution

*We Americans are the peculiar, the chosen
people—the Israel of our time; we bear the ark of
the liberties of the world.*

Herman Melville, *White Jacket*

*Sail, sail thy best, ship of democracy,
Of value is thy freight, 'tis not the Present only,
The Past is also stored in thee,
Thou holdest not the nature of thyself alone, not
    of the Western continent alone,
Earth's résumé entire floats on thy keel O ship, is
    steadied by thy spars,
With thee Time voyages in trust, the antecedent
    nations sink or swim with thee,
With all their ancient struggles, martyrs, heroes,
    epics, wars, thou bear'st the other continents,
Theirs, theirs as much as thine, the destination-
    port trumphant;
Steer then with good strong hand and wary eye O
    helmsman, thou carriest great companions,
Venerable priestly Asia sails this day with thee,
And royal feudal Europe sails with thee.*

Walt Whitman, "Thou Mother with thy Equal
    Brood" *Leaves of Grass*

*In democratic times enjoyments are more lively
than in times of aristocracy, and more especially,
immeasurably greater numbers taste them. But,
on the other hand, one must admit that hopes are
much more often disappointed, minds are more
anxious and on edge, and trouble is felt more
keenly.*

Alexis de Tocqueville, *Democracy in America*

HUMBERT REFLECTS

(more than twenty years on)

O my America   my new found land
once you were Lolita in her prime
(about eleven years) all innocent
and making love in mad motels with old
decrepit Europe   He with shaking hand
squeezed on your tiny breasts while all the time
you popped your gum   indifferent   intent
on making bubbles   rhythmically controlled
as were your pelvic movements   And the arse
of Humbert Europe flayed in desperation

O my America   where is your cool
your innocence   your gum   after the farce
of Vietnam has turned to hesitation
all the rude confidence only a fool
would underestimate
                      But now you are
snappy   defensive   almost middle-aged
a sad declining whore mourning her past
with petulant assertiveness
                      Your car
is Japanese   You drive but are enraged
Pearl Harbor was avenged   but now at last
they've hit you in the sagging underbelly
no credit cards can cure

                      You feel the strain
but   my once brash tart   are not prepared
(my glum Lolita sadly run to fat)
like an Imperial courtesan to maintain
a dignified indifference of the herd—

that jeering mob of nouveau powerful
who long to see you totter and fall flat
but haven't quite the courage yet to push

Well   somehow faded lady I shall pull
my own stiff joints erect and tip my hat
and gently help you through the vulgar crush—
stave off disaster for another hour—
and through your pouts and tempers try to see
nostalgic flashes of that innocence
that drove old Humbert crazy with desire
and then itself with pot and LSD
and indignation half devoid of sense

I'll stick around Lolita and I'll fill
the glasses for you for a little while
There's no where else to go   I had to come
and now I want to stay   But I'll not kill
to save your pride   or for your faded smile
Napalm tastes bad kid   should have stuck with gum

THE MARINE ROOM RESTAURANT

(of the Olympic Hotel, Seattle, Washington)

That genius for the oil-and-water mix
of careful taste and gross vulgarity
erupts in walls of living timelessness—
glass-prisoned   nervous fish   that stare at us
across a million centuries
                              The roof
is blue   the light subdued   the tables ranged
in tiers down to a pit   where girls on legs
serve passive actors of this aqueous scene
with whisky (sour)   and with martini (dry)
with maraschino (red)   and olive (green)

Some middle-income lumpen bourgeosie
celebrate the anniversarie
of legal coupling   while the silent fish
look on unmoved   but are not looked upon
Who needs the colored flame that burns in tanks
of violent green   pale coral   amber rock
for   with a painful suddenness   the band
strikes   and we are drowned with cool trombones

Light   noise   hysteria   and then—oh God—
straight from Las Vegas—can you bear to wait?
"The Happy Jesters!"
                      Three sad   ancient men
in powder blue and cloying harmony
pull faces   put on hats   rotate their hips
do imitations of old movie stars

Meanwhile ten thousand quiet   brilliant forms
swim round our heads   as we consume huge steaks

of local salmon (broiled)   with spinach (creamed)
freezing our faces tight against the din
But in the pit the celebrants are pleased
They shriek applause and touch each others hands

Did you   comrade   turn to me and say
(struggling through your pain to rationalize)
"It's good that we should be exposed to this
for this is real   and intellectuals
should know how people live and what they like"
You did
            But I had left you with the thought
that poor sweet Ludwig would have loved this room
and reproduced it on a mountain top
in warm Bavaria   There he and I
would flood the pit and all its ruminants
til they were happy   chomping   protean mud
churning to the sub-aquatic tones
of happy jesters and of sad trombones

Then in the swan boat on the lake we'd sit
and call up Parsifal from hidden choirs
eat cherries from a shallow   silver dish
and olives from a bowl of ivory
We'd scatter lilies to the mountain folk
who came to us for bread—yet loved us more
for flowers—and would die for us because
they know we are not mad   but half-divine
princes   who ripen olives with our gaze
who feed wild cherries to our hunting dogs
who feel the colored fish swim through our blood

WORDS FOR A BOSTON BLUES

(tune: St James' Infirmary)

(from a true incident, 1957)

I went down to Boston harbor
to see what I could see there
and down on the sidewalk was a black man   dead
and blood ran from his throat   and blood was in his hair

A white woman bending over him
her eyes were wet and she bowed her head
then she turned her face toward me
these were the words she said

"He loved me like a proper man
I loved him back like a woman should
now he lies on the sidewalk dead
but his blood is as red as a white man's blood"

These truths we hold self-evident
from them no turning back
that man is equal born to man
unless that man be black

I knew as I left the harbor
with the blood wet under my feet
that only cold black violence
could clean that bloody street

I came back from Boston harbor
was the hottest time of the year
a nation lay on the sidewalk there
it smelled of blood   and it smelled of fear

BORING CONFESSION

(written on napkins with a pencil borrowed from the waitress
in the Sandalwood Bar of the Sheraton Route 18 New Jersey)

When thick with hatred   usually I find
room for compassion   since I have been on
the receiving end of hatred   So when faced
with wall-to-wall vulgarity like this
            (must I describe it   you all know the scene)
I know that I would open up the cocks
and filled with mercy   flood the frantic mess
until its noisy pointlessness was drowned
in vodka clean with ice
                        (Somewhere before
        I had the same clear flash of cruelty
        Was it again because the band was bad
        and no one seemed to care   or even know?)
And furthermore   choked with distaste I'd feel
not even hatred but indifference
        (I never feel it in a truckers' bar
        when watching football   but I must confess
        I've felt it in Elaine's time or two)
Somehow their earnest striving to be more
than nothing   leaves me robbed   exhausted
of understanding   I'm afraid to know
that Dachau   was no accident   no work
of lunatics   (too easy an excuse)
I am not mad or blood-crazed   but I am
an Eichmann of the disco bars   a fool
appointed Gauleiter of Route 18

Which tells me something about evil   but
an intuition I cannot explore
without a terror of the truth   a truth

undoubtedly banal   (which doesn't help)
I stop   accept   I drink   I dance   I laugh
and contemplate the soft alternatives
of passive curiosity   the escape
into the luxury of explanation

I should avoid all petty pick-up bars
all disco bands   all orders of tequila
sunrise   dropped into the polyester
laps of nervous blacks and orientals
that hint of pogroms and the smoky end
of things that have no purpose but to live

(Distracted by the waitress   the boring confession
takes a conventionally romantic turn—which is
a bit of a relief but not much)

But somehow when she wanders through the bar
her hair falls like a mermaid's   and the tinsel
floats behind like seaweed   and her skin
is pure as pearls   She converts the noise
into the thunder of a distant wave
that only adds to intimacy in
the liquefying chamber that envelopes
bodies and minds in vodka teased with lime
and sharp with ice   Swirling into depths
of hair-blown   sea-borne fantasy   she calls
me to the whirlpool of the drowning mass
into the peace that lies beyond all bands
all turnpikes   surf-and-turf   all Paul Masson
all lobsters Newburg   broiled or thermidor
and in some corner of polluted earth
gives promise of a sea-floor walk beside
the living scarlet claws   the silver smelts
the shining sea-bass and the patient clams—
and quiet death amid the tangled hair

(This boring reverie breaks off   another napkin
is requested   and the confession continues its dreary
and self-indulgent examination of the obvious)

Somewhere in the pointless certainty
of knowing one's distaste lies the unease
that by some gross political mischance
an idiot democracy will   out of fear
elect one to effective execution
of just those gruesome prejudices   which
are best when least explored   and worst
when given self-expression in the name
of higher values   which one will accept
knowing that such acceptance must embrace
a sickness only violence can cure

God save us sinners from such expurgation
Leave the world's banal impurity
free from our outrage   noisily content

(Here   mercifully   we run out of napkins and the
waitress demands her pencil back)

FOR MY DAUGHTERS
(on the anniversary of the killings at Kent State, May 4, 1970)

I have dreams for you
cliché dreams little girls
dreams that father-everyman
has for daughter-everygirl
silly   romantic dreams

I would have you all
growing up in Georgian
houses in the summer
with beaches where your limbs
could test their firmness   crabs
in the pools and starfish and
colored rocks to puzzle
and intrigue   provoking
question after question

Careless hours stretching
through a carefree youth
with you all   all three
mad with the love of wind
of mountains and of donkeys
and of wolfhounds obedient
to your imperious little whims

Careless youth stretching
into grave   humorous   awkwardly
graceful ladyhood   My three
young ladies serious at the
table among the candles
and the silver and the

darting conversation
with question after question
with laughter   music   songs
with witty teasing words
for desperate young men
whom I would hate
                    This I
would have for you
                    But I
know where you would be
dressed in faded jeans
clinging to your friends
out on the grass unarmed
in tears of mad frustration
in bitter helplessness
in angry incoherence
screaming motherfucker
at the khaki   booted
untidy boys with rifles
itching for the chance
to pay you back the scorn
and fury you were spitting
not at them but at
the things their shaking rifles
stood for
                When they fired
and you turned and screamed
who would have died? My mind
is numb   One cannot bear
to contemplate the wretched
sick sad truth   and yet
some man's daughter died there
and were his dreams less precious
than my little dreams?

You would have been out there
in that sun before those
bayonets facing death
I would have died my own
cold death knowing that

nothing I had dreamed
for you could possibly
have equalled all your courage
knowing that I would be
passionately proud
and wide awake with no
dreams left   only a dead
reality and question
after question
                    You
cannot control the hounds
with all your innocence
and we wise dreamers fail
to curb the wolf with dreams
All I can give you now
serious   funny   girls
is question after question

LIBERATED WOMAN:
HAPPINESS PURSUED

*Poland's leaders still pinned their trust to the
value of a large mass of horsed cavalry, and cherished a pathetic belief in the possibility of carrying
out cavalry charges. In that respect, it might truly
be said that their ideas were eighty years out of
date, since the futility of cavalry charges had been
shown as far back as the American Civil War.*

B. H. Liddell Hart, *History of the Second
World War*

. . . .

She has no history   yet she claims a name
that   though distorted   conjures slavic woods
goose herders
                    vampires
                                trolls
                                        but does it mean
anything to her?
                    Nothing
                            Well   perhaps
the echoes of a grandparental song—
of half-lost recipes
                        She has no sense
of time
            Nothing connects
                                Eternally
she recreates time for herself
                                    creates
her own
            is never moved by things that loom

through eastern European mists like fears
from childhood
        "But" I say "the Poles were brave
creative   brilliant   stubborn"
              "Yes" she says
But nothing registers
        not even echoes

She is eternal in her innocence
free from the grubby thrill of wickedness
lacking a twitch of mild perversity
The only sin she'll recognize is guilt
Her sex is easy   frank   manipulative
without a shred of mystery
        It has
the Constitution's sweeping optimism
the brash assertion of the Declaration
a Bill of Rights for severing all ties
to feudal sex   to nature's bondage   or
to any *dro*it or *jus* seignorial
in nocte prima or on any night

The pill is her democracy   her right
to be the same to all men
        all who are
created equally between her legs
She has no lovers   only partners who
engage her in a ritualistic dance
which   she maintains   in any case is better
performed alone in terms of its effect
(the manuals on the subject all agree)
Even so   one tries to cultivate
healthy relationships   without demands
without those screaming shitty consequences

If she loses
        if it seems unsure
if nothing works
        if simple quantity
fails to produce the happiness that should

be guaranteed by the pursuit
                    she knows
it can be fixed in time
                    A formula
will soon be found to take advantage of
progressive technological advance
in sexual plumbing
                    or in counselling
relationships
                    and broken hopes
                              and lives
All present tense
                    There is no history
to conquer here   and nature   as she knows
is nurture's creature
                    nurture going wrong
the experts can be called to fix it up

Your body turns in space
                              no weight   no time
A sexual walk in space
                    Nothing connects
to blood and sperm
                    to death and ovulation
to stench of birth
                    to anguish of lost love
to race   to earth
                    A body stretched
in space   that only wracks itself and shakes
in quick convulsion if manipulated
expertly by experts
                    Not in time
or history   but simply floating there
orbiting around the guarantees
the founding partners wrote into the rules
of liberation   happiness   and life

But then you creep against me in the night
after the satisfaction and the frank
and full discussion of our needs

and how
the sudden pleasure can be best achieved
by slow   sequential   oral expertise
demanding nothing mutual
                              nothing fierce
no simultaneous nonsense
                              no vaginal
myths
          You curl your body into mine
and say "I love you"
                    half ashamed
                                        dismayed
admitting dirty thoughts your grandmother
had to endure in less enlightened times
of smoky kitchens
                    cabbage
                              brats
                                        and sweat

I look into those slavic eyes and see
reflected in the wild green distance
                              lines
of cavalry glide on their perfect charge
toward the German tanks
                    slashing with swords
against the indifferent steel
                              So what's the use
your ever plunging into history
to know why men would die to save their young
only to have the young die in their turn
to save the women who will die to save
their young who'll die to save the women
who will die . . .
                    Stay out in space my love
Call in the experts   let their skillful tongues
produce your sterile spasms
                              and be safe

I shall dream of death in battle
                              or

the anguish of lost love
                        the agony
of childbirth and the death of children
                                    or
the fierceness of possession
                            or the hate
that is the kissing cousin of our loves
I'll dream
            of retrograde   archaic things
of bloody   unenlightened things
                            while you
are safe
        in space
                inviolate
                        satisfied

MANHATTAN SUMMER DIALOGUE: STATEN ISLAND INTERLUDE

I am about to sacrifice the dear little divine thing from among the mountains. My friends and masters, come to the feast!

O Divine One, you were sent into this world for us to hunt. When you come to them, the spirits, please speak well of us and tell them how kind we have been. Please come to us again and we shall do you the honor of a sacrifice.

Prayer to the sacrificial bearcub
Kyosuki Kindaiti, *Ainu Life and Legends*

The location of the sites in remote caves, where they would be most readily concealed, indicated their reference to a cult; and so it immediately occured to their excavators that they were uncovering the evidences of a sacrificial offering, storage places of the cave-bear skulls used in a service honoring the divinity of the hunt, to whom the offerings were rendered.

Such details among the contemporary Asiatic hunters as the grinding down of the teeth of the bear and leaving of two vertebrae attached to the skull, just as in the European Inter-glacial period, proves that the continuity has actually remained unbroken for tens of thousands of years.

Herbert Kühn "Das Problem des Urmonotheismus"
(translated by Joseph Campbell)

. . . .

I

He   There must be more bad guitarists per square mile
in Washington Square
than anywhere
on earth   Why do you smile?
Agree or strongly disagree? It isn't clear

She   In Staten Island Zoo there's an old bear
He's sad and grumpy   but he likes to hear
me   and me only
playing the guitar
Badly   He really is that lonely

He   Is it far
to Staten Island?   Perhaps the bear
(are you sure he doesn't smell?)
would like my conversation just as well
as your guitar   Even if I talk
badly   With bears of course one cannot tell

She   If we could walk
we'd go through Chinatown and we'd collect
(I know where they are sold)
little lanterns   red and gold
to hang up in the zoo
to please the prisoners   But I expect
that is forbidden   Most things are

He   What we could do
since we've just met and I don't even know your name
only that you
and I are no way   no way the same
is go to Chinatown and eat

She   It must be something without meat

He   O.K.   Then to the zoo

She   Then to the zoo   We'll take the Ferry   Have you got a car?
      It really isn't far

II

She   When they take the nests to make the soup
      what do the birds do?

He   The birds have long since gone
      in a wild   wheeling   cackling troop
      to find the sun or something   Very few
      care much about their nests or what goes on
      when they have left
      They have poor memories for little things
      but memories as wide as heaven and as loud
      as the beating of their million million wings
      for distances that Caravelles can't fly
      for every star and cloud
      that in the sky
      of southern summers points the way
      to that red lantern-lighted land
      of near-eternal golden day
      And you must understand
      they don't then mind the theft
      of little nests to feed those hungry girls
      who need their strength for serenading bears

She   Is all that true?
      That garbage about birds I mean?
      About the bears I know
      They never go
      anywhere

They live in holes alone   except
when mating for a while
Now it's your turn to smile
but I have been
in my hole alone just like the bear

He   Now you have crept
      outside to mate?

She A bit too late
      perhaps   And yet perhaps
      What garbage
      all that stuff about the birds

III

She They always miss—
      the ferry men   despite
      the years and years they've done it
      always hit
      the wall as they come in
      I'll blow a kiss
      to that big sad one there
      The one that looks just like a bear
      It gives him such a fright
      Is that a sin?
      I was brought up a Catholic

He   And now you worship bears?

She No   I don't worship anything anymore
      I just don't eat meat
      and sing to bears   (it's all the poor thing's got)
      I venerate them like the Virgin Mary   not
      worship them like Christ   That's neat

remembering things like that from long before
I ever sang to bears on Staten Island

He   Can't be long
You can't be more
than seventeen or eighteen

She   Well there you're wrong
I'm nineteen
and it is a hell of a long
time   a hell of a long time
since Long Island City
and my mother   and my sisters   and the pretty
dresses worn to Sunday mass
before I went into my hole
and venerated bears
and committed what was then
as far as I could see the only crime—
enjoying sex with men
So I went mad with men   I used to pray
I'd have two every day
I nearly made it   Never had affairs
You know   long-lasting stuff
until this recent guy   and that was rough
I liked him   but it's over   and again
Give Us This Day Our Daily Men
They said I'd lose my soul
those Catholics
But my mother was half Jewish so I guess
I got off to a rotten start
as far as those things were concerned   What a crazy mess
a kosher sacred heart
a Catholic quarter Jew
And quit your laughing   What the hell are you?

He   God knows
A Deist I suppose
One who chooses to believe
that God exists   the better for to hate
my dear Him for his ravages   Doglike to bait

133

Him the great   immortal   pompous beast
with bestial snarls and yelps of sheer
defiance   or at least
to weave
some fantasies like this to pass the year
we seem to be spending getting off this raft

She   What garbage   I guess I should have laughed
You should take care
God just might be a bear
He did once leave
his hole in heaven to come down and mate
Just once   I think that's great
But you should venerate
the Great God Bear   This is the gate

He   You didn't bring your bad guitar
to serenade him

She   Well   what was the use
the bear was an excuse
He's locked up for the night
But there is still some light
and lots of time to kill
So chase me round these trees
and if you catch me   which you will
we'll go down on our knees
with hands behind our backs and kiss
like children do in China

He   Out of breath   I'm not nineteen and I
am out of breath   But with enough
to kiss under a Chinese lantern sky
a grim polluted golden red
I couldn't miss
You let me catch you

She   Well now   Ain't that tough
Of course I did   So now let's kiss
for five full minutes   Understand

you mustn't use a hand
I am too young
to have my innocent body violated thus
So use your tongue
and gorge yourself on my young mouth
and think of us
as Chinese children learning what it's like
to kiss for the first time   Open your mouth

He   Was that five minutes

She   I don't want a quiz
Do as I tell you
Take my hand and run

He   Well   What's done is done
and now I must obey
the priestess of the bear

She   Come out this way
and over there
you'll see somewhere
in the filthy   fading light
of our Staten Island night
if I have not
forgotten   there behind the parking lot
a hill   A long   steep   roughly sloping hill
That's where we'll run   where you and me will
roll down together   locked together tight
Have you ever rolled like that before?

He   Certainly not   and what is more
It's bound to be against the law
All such things are   Hills
are not made for rolling   not these hills
They're made as landscape features   made to ease
the lot of weary motorists   not made to please
bear goddesses who tease
susceptible old deists   Merciful God
You can't be serious?

135

She   Do you want to make love with me?

He   What else   Of course
       I've thought of little else for six hours now
       since we met up in town

She   Then you must roll with me and when we're down
      among the garbage   hidden from the cars
      then you can have me any way you want
      under your clumsy God's polluted stars

IV

She   You need my hand
      to lead you to the promised land?
      But first   like Pilgrim   you must climb this hill
      which will
      prove how much you want me

He   You mustn't taunt
      A pilgrimage is such a serious thing
      and if I'm to do my Pilgrim thing
      then let me do it with some dignity

She   O.K.   Then sing
      a solemn song about eternity
      and bird nest soup   and bears
      bored out of their minds by bad guitars
      Let's have few   sad   squeaky bars

He   For Christ's sake stop
      we're at the bloody top
      What now?   Do I ascend
      into a special heaven full of holes

for timid bears afraid to mate
with other timid souls?

She   Why no   You fall
This is the fall of woman and of man
the ending of my innocence
Lie down and hold me tight   tight as you can
Now there is no pretense
Your bluff is called old pilgrim   Now you will
roll with me down this hill

He   When I recall
this day to my grandchildren
who will ask
"When the world trembled grandpa   what
did you do   What was your great task?"
I'll tell them   "Not a lot
I rolled down hills a bit with crazy bears"

She   You talk a lot of garbage
You talk a lot
So let's get rolling if you want me hot

    The spinning trees   the red
and gold revolving sky
the frightened birds that crashed
upward through turning
branches as we flashed
a barrel headlong burning
an avalanche of legs and hair
a long dress torn   a shattered
watch   a sandal shed
left lying there
not that it mattered
as down and round and down and round
down round down we sped
until we hit the ground
among the garbage   hidden from the cars
and all the grimy stars

stopped spinning   and our bodies bruised
and winded   lay there waiting to be used

She   Now   Now   For God's sake now
Don't wait a second   Do it anyhow
Just pound and crush me like the hill
has nearly crushed us both   Hard   Hard   I will
not want it in a second   Now   Now   Now

V

She   They'll hit it going this way too
They always do
My God that was a crazy screw
I often have aesthetic orgasms   you know
I come just out of joy   like when
lighting a Chinese lantern   by its glow
I look into the river   Or when men
lick their lips and look me up and down
I had one when we met in town
and you gave me all the crazy talk
and on the walk
to find the crazy bear
who I knew would not be there
I have them when I see a sexy black
I have them all the time when things
are beautiful   A nymphomaniac
for beauty's what I am
Or a rotten sham
Nothing rings
true

He   Do you often do
what we just did?

She   Hell no
      A long   long time ago
      I rolled that hill with someone just
      like you   and for the same   same reason

He   Your own form of lust
      in your own mating season?
      An aphrodysiacal tumble for a kid
      who otherwise has only superficial
      orgasms by the dozen in the street?

She   Oh man   That's neat
      That's psychological
      That's really neat
      But what we did
      I did for the same reason once before
      I only ever did it once before
      I hope I never do it anymore
      And you should know the score
      the outcome   rolling lover   of what you did
      I want it beautiful   you see
      And I should know
      because to make the kid
      was beautiful   the one I'm three
      months pregnant with   And when it goes
      when I abort it as you'd say
      I want it the same way
      So thanks   You did it beautifully friend
      Now I'll wait for the end
      alone   down in my hole
      I don't think I ever had a lousy soul

HYMN TO ISIS:
SAN FRANCISCO SUMMER

. . . .

From D. H. Lawrence, *The Man Who Died*

"I serve Isis in search," she replied.
He looked at her. She was like a soft musing cloud, somehow remote.
His soul smote him with passion and compassion.
"Mayst thou find thy desire, maiden," he said, with sudden earnestness.
"And art thou not Osiris?" she asked.
He flushed suddenly.
"Yes, if thou wilt heal me!" he said. "For the death aloofness is upon me, and I cannot escape it."

PREAMBLE: SAN FRANCISCO SUMMER AFTERNOON

The hippie girl was pale with sickness and
had long   uncertain hair
I touched her shaking hand
and kissed the flowers painted on
her cheeks   which   death inspired   shone
through primary blue and red
with luminous   Pre-Raphaelite effect

Flowers painted on a rocking horse
Ophelia's flowers   she being almost dead
Flowers that Victorian girls collect

140

to dry and press and torment   all of course
to make such pretty pictures   This remorse
is premature

She slowly lifts her head
and with my finger tips
I gently trace round purple lips
round earrings carved from oriental creeds
mandalas   wampum collars   amber beads
that hang like crystal sweat across her brow

Again she lifts her head   and now
with fingers sliding through her anxious hair
I kiss the painted stars around her eyes
while peeping through her drug-dulled stare
a childish hope discredits her disguise

She tells me how
she knows that as she lives she dies
but   she never thinks of death
despite her illness and her cough
though these remind her   Still   she shrugs it off
and hides behind a cloud of smoky breath

She tells me that the door would never lock
puts on a record   joins in with the song
She lights the incense   strokes a joint with long
uncertain fingers   serves tea and brown rice
then sits   a lotus   on the floor again
and lets the music carved from hardened rock
cut like obsidian through her waking brain

　　　Music that harsher on the spirit lies
　　　than painted eyelids upon smoke-filled eyes

　　　Music that strains
　　　　　　　　　　　and strains
　　　　　　　　　　　　　　　　and falling
　　　　　　　　　　　　　　　　　　　dies

INCIDENT IN THE UNCONSCIOUS
(with apologies to A.C.S.)

Her eyes are the eyes of hunted doe
   and I am haunted   taunted   though
by a need unspoken   a seal unbroken
   a memory hidden   a thought forbidden
a forest footfall   a frightened breath
   a murmur of blood   a whisper of death
of eyes that are mingling fear and trust
   of hands that are mangling love and lust

The loud voice screams   "You must answer her need"
   The soft voice answers   "Greed   greed   greed"
But the goddess pursuing the missing part
   finds the Maenad tearing a young god's heart
And that which was whole is rent in twain
   and that which was sundered is sought in vain
and the blood is washed from the leaves by the rain
   while the voice of the forest cries   "Pain   pain   pain"

S.F. SUMMER AFTERNOON—CONT.

She talks a lot about herself and how
sex is for her an agreeable device
for exploring meaningful relationships
at worst quite bearable   at best quite nice
and healthy   like brown rice
not bad for you like other trips
and much the best when high
with a casual passerby

but in itself no end
a service to a friend
perhaps   to pass the time

and on and on and on
until the afternoon was gone
the San Francisco summer afternoon was gone

Then she says   (to be polite)
"You'd like to stay the night?
I get a very definite vibration
from your Victorian imagination
that I turn on to   Is it sex-and-crime—
a Jack the Ripper thing?   I'm screwing all the time

I guess I do it just to pass the time
It's like   well   good   but not great anytime
I mean   I've never had that final screw turned tight
You know   the one that might
just make me scream
but that's my dream
You're gonna stay the night?"

Loud voice   "Do it   It is right"
Soft voice   "Greed   greed   greed"

She looked at him for a moment in fear, from the soft blue sun of her
eyes. Then she lowered her head, and they sat in silence in the warmth
and glow of the western sun: the man who had died, and the woman of
the pure search.

STATEMENT OF INTENT

No
She must be freed
Teach her to embrace pain as a friend
that she might know sex as an end
and both as means to nothing
but a meaningful relationship
of celebrants in that fierce rite
which is but an echo of the end
a shadow on a smoky summer night
a cheap rehearsal of the end
when that last   agonizing screw turns tight

So
When
floating through the amber fire of pain
(God's golden arrow through that mad saint's heart)
at last I enter   then
her frantic fingernails
I'm certain will
respond with quick   instinctive skill
clawing release from those indulgent jails
of all-too-easy sex   cancelling
the life-destroying message of the pill

The final turn   And then there is the note
of silent screaming somewhere in her throat

My torn flesh will sing
to me that all is gain
Her painted eyes
calm now beyond all pain
are smudged with stinging sweat
and yet
are penitent and wise
She will rise
moving to different music now

with certain pace
and all the oriental grace
for which she longs
and makes her like Diana of the Chase
queen of herself
and of all moonlight things
that move as underwater to the sound
of temple gongs
from cities drowned
a million years ago

When she sings
the chant will be melodious and slow
The notes will be the rain
on bars of moonlight
There will be no strain
only as from a distant height
the echo of a liquefying pain
a rainwashed forest filled with blood and pain
drowned in the moonlight and reborn again

THE HYMN TO ISIS

Isis
now you have Osiris whole
Having found a grip
foreswear another sterile trip
into that colored fairyland
whose gainless occupation
is rhythmic   dull   ingenious copulation
Isis
let my torn body be your goal
for now you understand
love is not easy   and warm Lethe's mud
is mud despite its psychedelic hue
Isis
we have reserved for you
passage on a lengthy Stygian trip
in Charon's dark   unhurried ship
The view of death is clear
the transformation imperceptible
Isis
there   as we live   we die
and passionately try
to make the art of death perfectible
and so the art of love   and we are high
only on the acid of our blood

She turned to him, her face glowing from the goddess.
"You are Osiris, aren't you?" she said naively.
"If you will," he said.
"Will you not let Isis discover you? Will you not take off your things?"
He looked at the woman, and lost his breath. And his wounds, and especially the death wound through his belly, began to cry again . . .
"They did me to death!" he said in excuse of himself, turning his face to her for a moment.
And she saw the ghost of the death in him, as he stood there thin and stark before her, and suddenly she was terrified, and she felt robbed. She felt the shadow of the gray, grisly wing of death triumphant.

ENVOI: SAN FRANCISCO SUMMER NIGHT

"You'll stay then   stay the night?"
"Well   well you know I'd like to   but you see
I've this appointment   and
I hope you understand
I can only stay an hour
Business   I must shave and shower
I hadn't planned . . ."

"O.K.   What the hell
an hour will do as well"

Well
It was nice
She said   "Man   that was nice"
I laughed and said   "Perhaps I'll make you scream
next time I'm here"
Her eyes were dull again   too dull for fear
She took another drag   She said   "Screw that old dream
I won't be here"   She said   "I won't be here"

I got my plane
I never went again

But now at night my sleepless hours
are filled with painted stars   and dying flowers

She never wrote   but in the end
I got a letter from a friend
in San Francisco
Shit
You all know what it said

INDIAN GIRL

(written in European exile)

What made the Mongols flee the East
the Huns to start their westward surge
the Celts to scatter 'til they ceased
their wanderings   but retained the urge?

What sent the Jews and Moors to Spain
and seaward rolled the restless herd
of Goths and Vandals   what again
in Cabot and Vespuggi stirred?

What wind sent Vikings to their death
and bishops to St. Brandon's Isle
and blew them with its scented breath
to doomed Atlantis for a while?

What fascination drew each rogue
and pious pilgrim to the West
sent Ossian down to Tir na n-Og
and even now denies me rest?

What set the trireme's groping oars
to fight Atlantic waves and win
sent men from Tyre to Albion's shores—
the mere excuse of Cornish tin?

Cynics   do not call it greed
this mad desire to track the sun
it is a much more ancient need
that seizes us and makes us run

It is the voice the migrant bird
feels urgent in its blood each year

It is the call Columbus heard
it is not greed   it is not fear

not power nor the hope of gain
(though motives such as these   one finds
make it much easier to explain
the strange intent to little minds)

Whatever is the movement's source
that drove those maniacs to the sea
I only know you are the force
the magnet that is drawing me

that you were there before the ships
before the bishops   pirates   kings
and what they sought is in your lips
is in the song your body sings

is in the rhythm of your drum
is in the patience of your eyes
is in the melody you hum
to coax the rain from desert skies

For you   my Pocahontas   were
princess of all   and you are still
your skin is yet the puma's fur
your breasts are each a sacred hill

your hair the trailing thundercloud
your smell the pinyon and the sage
your pride a wind-torn pine unbowed
your anger is the cyclone's rage

A towering mesa is your scorn
a colored canyon is your love
into whose depths we have been drawn
indifferent to the storm above

Yet it is shrieking overhead
a challenge to our stubborn wills

and when its snarling voice is dead
we feel the silence of the hills

We hear the mad coyote's cry
the warning rattle in the dust
The eagle's wings obstruct the sky
and fear destroys our waning lust

fear that none of this was meant
that we are prisoners of time
your body is the continent
we merely re-enact the crime

Our mutual passion comes too late
to heal the wounds of centuries
to reconcile the love and hate
inherent in such loves as these

And though I know our love is doom
(the love that drove those pirates   kings
and bishops to their watery tomb)
I crave the danger that it brings

For still you are the desert moon
that draws the tidal wave in me
towards the West   and very soon
I'll cross the inevitable sea

Four

Toward

a More

Perfect

Dissolution

He knows that there was once an ice age and that there will be an ice age again.

George Wyndham on A. J. Balfour

WHAT CAN BE DONE ABOUT SWEDEN?

> *And now what shall become of us without any barbarians?*
> *Those people were a kind of solution.*
>
> C. P. Cavafy, "Expecting the Barbarians"

. . . .

Extract from a speech to the United Nations' Committee on the Problems of the Overdeveloped Countries, by the head of the UN Investigative Commission on Sweden, the Ambassador from Uganda.

. . . have occupied this distinguished body for some time. But before getting as quickly as possible to the substance of my report and recommendations, I must ask for the patience of the assembly while I indulge in a little custom of my country where no one begins a speech to the "great council"—as we would call such an august body as this—without having the courtesy to tell what we would call a "little tale" or "small story." This is done—according to western anthropologists, who, of course, understand our customs better than we do ourselves (*laughter*) in order to make the assembled distinguished company feel "at home" as you would say, and less intimidated by the awesomeness of the occasion (*laughter*). The little story, as is our custom, is usually a small anecdote from the life of the speaker, and since we, that is our team of investigators, have just returned from Sweden—that unhappy, ravaged land—my story will concern my reaction to my first real view of Stockholm. This was from the beautiful dining room at the top of the tallest bank building in that beautiful city. The room had once been the apartment of the chancellor of the royal household, and our most gracious and kind hosts had pointed with pride to a window in the apartment that was bricked up and had been since the eighteenth century—the era of the said chancellor. The window faced onto the royal palace across the water, and the distressed man so hated his work that when he returned home in the evening he could not bear to look at the palace—hence the bricks

155

(*laughter*) that had been left there, in his memory, ever since. But that is not my little tale. From the unbricked windows there was the most beautiful view of this "Venice of the north"—its lakes, inlets, bridges, palaces, cathedrals, parks, avenues. Even in the admittedly pale sunlight it was a superb sight. But something about it disturbed me. In the course of my peripatetic European education, gentlemen, I visited all the capitals of Europe collecting four doctorates en route. Something about this capital, however, struck me as odd, but I could not think at first what it was. At least I knew what struck me, but could not at first think why it was odd! *Everything was intact exactly as it had been built* (*murmurs*). A fifteenth-century church was still there—perfect. A seventeenth-century palace was in the same condition as when built. An eighteenth-century cathedral was there as it stood at its completion. A nineteenth-century Opera House: in pristine condition. And the thought that struck me, that tied together the "oddness" of it all? Gentlemen, I confess that I turned to my charming host and exclaimed, "Why, this city has never been bombed; it has *never* been bombed!" (*murmurs, some slight laughter*)

It is the custom in my country—and I was naughty not to tell you this before—that the little tale should have a moral (*laughter*) but that the moral should never be revealed (*more laughter*). In this case, gentlemen, the moral is not in need of revelation. You are all aware of the grave situation in Sweden and the reason why our intervention was required and requested. The Third World Commission on the Problems of Over-developed Countries has been, to say the least, overworked of late—and as you know overwork is one of the early symptoms of overdevelopment, so we must be more careful (*more laughter*)—but work we must and work we will as long as the grave situation in the overdeveloped countries persists and as long as we have the means and the will to come to their aid (*prolonged applause*).

Nor do I need to bore you with a repetition of the long diagnosis—nay the many diagnoses—that have been offered this distinguished assembly on the problems of overdevelopment. Sweden, as you know, was very special since it had been dismissed by many sceptics as a hopeless case. Social justice was perfect—both legal justice and "distributive" justice; social welfare had reached the limits of its possibilities as a result of 90 percent taxation returned largely in the form of benefits; the criminal justice system was the most "enlightened" in the world, and rehabilitation was totally substituted for retribution in all spheres; the standard of living was the highest in the world; sexual liberty was in its most advanced stages; war was outlawed and neutrality the national policy . . . I could go on, but these, as we all know, are the sure signs of hyper-advanced overdevelopment, with their concomitants of severe alcoholism, staggering rates of suicide and mental breakdown—especially clinical depression, and "motiveless" crimes including sexual offenses quite unnecessary in a country of such permissiveness. And this very permissiveness is indicative of the chronic nature of the problem. This did not originate as it would have done in any normal country from an overflow of natural lust (*laughter*) but derived from a puritanical thoroughness in teaching sexual hygiene to young schoolchildren such that they could not, when adult, properly distinguish sexual intercourse from good dental care, and evaluated each about as exciting as the other. Need I add that large scale epidemics of impotence have been reported and the situation is growing graver by the hour (*murmurs*).

No. I shall not bore the distinguished gathering with the details and diagnoses: severe overdevelopment is too obvious to need much analysis. When the house is on fire, you put the fire out, you do not discourse on the theory of heat (*laughter*). I shall proceed therefore to the recommendations that your commission proposed as immediate measures to be taken to "stop the rot." Whether the situation can ever be reversed is not clear, but we must always try my colleagues, must we not? We must always hope (*applause*).

The overall principle which has guided us in this as in all previous cases (our modest success in West Germany can be cited) is the introduction of a sufficient measure of social injustice and communal chaos to restore normal human functionings. Of course, this has to be attuned to the particular conditions of the country concerned, but the following are what we suggest as at least interim measures in the case of this unfortunate northern paradise.

1. The Mafia should be introduced at once and should infiltrate the trade unions and the herring industry. Gambling casinos should be opened and a number of bankers corrupted to the point where they "make deals" with the mob. Judges and ministers should be bribed and a steady run of scandals in high places should be instituted.

2. Stockholm should be bombed.

3. About 400,000 of the Mexicans now flooding into the United States should be diverted to Sweden. They should be immediately put in charge of the postal services, and any other bureaucratic services where strict adherence to the Protestant Ethic is at present required. A bull ring should be set up in Uppsala.

4. The Swedes have already shown an admirable capacity for racist attitudes. It is your committee's feeling that these indigenous strengths should be capitalized on in all possible cases. Too often "aid" from the

outside fails because it does not tap these indigenous motivations (*applause*). Thus we recommend that about two million black people should be sent immediately from some of the starving nations of the world. This will be a sacrifice for them, but their better impulses could be appealed to. Perhaps we could form an international "chaos corps?" I know my own countrymen would not flinch from their duty to the less fortunate in this respect (*applause*).

5. The above assistance would have a double effect. Not only would it introduce massive racial unrest as competition for jobs got underway, but the well-known penchant of Swedish women for black males would introduce an element of vicious sexual competition, which should cure the impotency problem overnight. The retaliation of the black women should prove an interesting experiment in its own right that might give us insights into how we might use this device elsewhere.

6. A border dispute with Finland should be provoked as soon as possible. Neutrality may not last if what has come to be known as "the territorial imperative" is threatened. If the Finnish government could be persuaded to maltreat the numerous Swedes living within its borders, this would help enormously.

7. Fornication outside legal marriage should be made a crime punishable by public flogging. Life imprisonment for adultery, and shooting for the distribution of pornography should be put on the statute books. All these sexual cases should be handled by highly vindictive ecclesiastical courts.

8. Prohibition should be introduced at once; preferably by a team of advisors from the USA to ensure maximum inefficiency. Sufficient supplies, however, should be left intact for Mafia-run bootlegging purposes.

9. The income tax should be abolished along with most social services. A strong monarchist party should take power.

10. Ingmar Bergman should be allowed to make a staggeringly boring, highly symbolic movie of the results—with Spanish subtitles.

As with all bold moves to alleviate the problems of overdevelopment, this one has its dangers. The Swedes may already be too mentally undernourished to respond at all to these generous infusions of aid. But, gentlemen, we must try, try, and try again. Our moral obligations to the less fortunate of the world do not admit us to utter the word "impossible." Thank you gentlemen for your indulgence. I respectfully submit the commission's report and urge speedy implementation (*prolonged applause, cheers, waving of papers, etc., etc.*).

IMAGE DE LA COMTESSE

Quand je regarde ce visage
Je sais
Que je ne suis pas raisonnable
(croyance incroyable)
Ca me dérange peut-être mais
Je suis quand même un fou bien sage
au moins
Je me battrais pour ce visage

Quand je regarde ce visage
je pense
Que je ne pourrais jamais être
de moi-même le maitre
(incroyable cette croyance)
car asservi par cette image
enfin
je tuerais pour ce visage

When I look at this face/I know/that I am not rational/(unbelievable belief)/this bothers me perhaps and yet/I am even so a pretty wise fool/at least/I would fight for this face.

When I look at this face/I think/that I could never be/master of myself/(unbelievable this belief)/because enslaved by this picture/in the end/I would kill for this face.

Quand je regarde ce visage
je crains
qu'il ne soit un agent du Diable
(croyance 'peu pres croyable)
Vous vous me rendrez dans ses mains
ou ebloui par l'esclavage
content
je mourrais donc pour ce visage

Quand je regarde ce visage
je crois
qu'il fait des mots de Dieu une fable
(incroyance bien croyable)
Prince infernal écoutez moi
Ecoutez aussi l'entourage
mon âme
je la vendrais pour ce visage

When I look at this face/I fear/that it's an agent of the devil/(belief almost believable)/ you give me up into his hands/where blinded by the slavery/happily/I would then die for this face.

When I look at this face/I believe/it makes the words of God a fiction/(pretty believable unbelief)/Prince of Darkness listen to me/you followers listen too/my soul/I would sell it for this face.

INTUITION, STRUCTURE, AND PASSION REVISITED

. . . .

LOVE AT FIRST SIGHT

Although I never saw your face before
your image was prefigured in my mind
assuring me that one day I could draw
upon this template   knowing I would find
with instant recognition what I sought
So when you blazed into my consciousness
the golden message in my brain was caught
examined   and in milliseconds   "yes"
came back the answer   "this is she who was
and is   and always will be coded there"
I did not need to verify because
the answer was confirmed by your brief stare
    And for one terrifying moment we
    were locked in perfect mental symmetry

STRUCTURAL SONNET

I cannot   by summation of each part
imply the living magic of the whole
That would require a logic of the heart

a limpid mathematics of the soul—
to grasp at once the juncture of green eyes
(that flash like timid emeralds in the night)
with an outrageous nose   to emphasize
the mouth when laughter sets the face alight
to witness that sharp movement of the head
so quick that it eludes the startled hair
and find for these a formula instead
to generate the surface magic there
    Then   through its transformations I would see
    the structure of my love's mythology

SONNET OF THE DARK LADY

In search of death from gentleness   in search
of those extremes that free us from the bonds
of little life   to worship in the church
of savage flesh whose rites demand the fronds
still wet with blood from that dark forest where
your eyes are green   then blue   then vacant black
(matching the peat-pool darkness of your hair)
until the python slides across your back
and round my thighs   and tightens its embrace
with slow unyielding torture   Then your eyes
are blazing sapphires burning through your face
and we are one with serpent   teeth   and thighs
    accepting pain and death with perfect trust
    crushed   and devoured by the snake of lust

SAD SONNET
(written in Bradley's, Greenwich Village,
with Rodrigo, improbably, on the juke box) *

Lack of you turns from numbness to despair
Neither guitars nor beer can ease the pain
With blatant sentiment that seems unfair
Rodrigo tears the guts from me again
Every female movement that's not yours
now tortures me   because I know I need
that warmth   that sensuous blindness   all that draws
my hungry mouth to fasten and to feed
My flesh irradiates the droning bar
until it drowns the gestures and the eyes
and old Rodrigo and the sad guitar
become mere adjuncts to my body's cries
    I stop my ears against these carnal moans
    and long for Satie's disembodied tones

*Actually, what was probably on the box was Miles Davis and his spooky trumpet version;
but recollecting in tranquility as I sketched this out on the back of a coaster, what I heard in
my head was the guitar concerto.

DESIGN FAILURE
A Post-tutorial Dialogue

*Metaphysics and the human sciences are made
impossible by the penetration of morality into the
moment to moment conduct of ordinary life: the
understanding of this fact is religion.*

Iris Murdoch, *The Philosopher's Pupil*

*We have just enough Religion to make us hate, but
not enough to make us love one another.*

Jonathan Swift, *Thoughts on Various Subjects*

. . . .

. . . which leaves Spinoza and Schopenhauer with much the same position: no free will however you look at it.

A nice paper. A sound conclusion.

You agree then? Your pessimism is like Schopenhauer's; at least Spinoza had the consolation of some kind of god.

I'm not sure that agreeing or disagreeing is what I should do—in my role as tutor. I should assess your argument, comment on its logic, your use of sources . . .

Oh come on! We can go off the record—as it were, as you would say.

Of course—as it were.

Then we have no free will—except the contemplation of necessity. We *are* determined. What is more, we are determined to self-destruct—if you'll forgive the confusion of meanings.

Forgiven. Since we are off the record let's say "doomed to self-destruct" and have done with it.

Because of innate aggressivity?

We've gone beyond that simple-minded kind of thinking—I hope! We

164

never had it really; it was how opponents phrased it, not us. A straw man. Innate aggressivity can be used for constructive as well as destructive ends. That's not what inspires my pessimism about Man's fate—forgive the pomposity.

Forgiven. But is there a greater justification for pessimism now than before?

Yes. Although the tendency to self-destructiveness was there, it did not previously have the means to destroy the whole species.

Is this tendency a product of modern technology, or is it endemic?

It is endemic—for reasons we can explore. But it need not have reached this pass. That it might do so was always *possible:* modern technology makes it probable. The probability increases daily.

Can science not save us?

No, because it too is at the heart of the problem. It should be what saves us, but it cannot act independently. It only acts in terms of values—judgements. These it makes very badly—a result of the design failure.

Why design failure? We were not designed.

No, but suppose we were (as some religions suppose). Would a superior intelligence have designed us the way we are? Only science fiction seems to have explored this, but it is at once our interest and our weakness that we seem to be somehow wrongly put together. God was in too much of a hurry to create in his own image. He missed.

Why did this hypothetical God miss?

Because he tried to fuse together a unique form of intelligence with a rather untried raw material—the evolving hominid. The result was a self-destructive mixture.

But if we were not in fact "designed," how did this really happen?

By an evolutionary accident. To become good at what we were doing we evolved this intelligence (or rather natural selection favored it). But having got it, it proved too powerful for its owner.

How can that be? Surely evolution does not go in for such excesses?

All the time—like the size of the dinosaurs, but not usually with intelligence—that was the error. A very different kind of feedback is set up.

How does this work to our disadvantage?

At first it didn't. Quite the contrary. The extra quality of this intelligent awareness enabled us to become top of the food chain. We should have stopped there.

Why didn't we—I mean, quit while we were ahead?

It is a peculiarity of this intelligence that it *cannot stop*. It started as simply a useful evolutionary device to help us adapt successfully—like speed, strength, etc. But it had one huge weakness.

What was that?

It knew what it was doing and it was curious about what more it could do.

Why is that bad?

Because it changed all the rules of the adaptive game. Animals do what they have to do. This animal asked: why am I doing it; perhaps I could do it better?

But surely it isn't a mistake to do better?

Yes it is. The point of adaptation is to do just as well as is necessary to adapt. An adaptation does not question itself: weight does not question weight, size does not question size, nor flight, flight. But consciousness questions consciousness. That is the beginning of the end—which came rather rapidly really.

But haven't we been evolving for millions of years?

And intelligently conscious for probably less than one of those. That is a very short run in evolutionary terms. But the run is really even shorter. Until about the end of the upper paleolithic, conscious intelligence was an adaptive aid. Then, given some unprecedented good weather, it was able to expand. The rundown has taken at best 10,000 years.

But surely in that time we did not decline, we improved—civilization, technology, science, art, etc?

Not really. Until the industrial revolution nothing very basic changed. Look at the cave painting of the upper paleolithic; study the religious ideas of primitive tribes—we have not improved on these. We changed in scale and appearance, but not in skill and intelligence. It was variations on a theme.

But since the industrial revolution?

Science is the ultimate intellectual curiosity. That has made the difference. But it was only intended as a handmaiden of values, which themselves spring from the needs of survival. It was never intended to have an independent existence, and has never really had one. The problem is its very success. It is still the handmaiden of values, and these have not changed—merely become inappropriate in the new environment that they and science have created.

Are you suggesting that we should have stayed as stone-age hunters?

In some senses, yes. But here is the basic problem: the very mechanism that enabled us to be successful hunters was way in excess of its needed capacity. This is where the positive feedback came in: better brains—more intelligence—set up conditions that needed even better brains to survive, and so on. The process was too rapid. The result was a sophisticated computer built into an emotional ape.

Surely the computer could control the ape?

Not really. There was control in the sense that the ape could now do his angry (and other) things more effectively. But the computer itself did not give any directions—it only followed. And the programming had to come from the raw material of the ape in question: a volatile, aggressive, vain, sentimental, greedy, cowardly, suspicious, loving mix-up of a creature.

But if it could do all these things better . . .?

Yes—sometimes it would work, but only under rather restricted conditions, namely those which it had evolved to cope with—small-scale hunting groups spread out over a rich environment. Once this scale was left behind, the great danger arose: the creature could start to design its own environment.

Why is that so bad?

It didn't know what to design. It was at the mercy of its own imagination, its own inventiveness. The computer was called upon more and more and seemed limitless in its capacity to invent more and more ingeniously. But no one knew why, except that it was worth doing for its own sake; because that is what it did.

But you said that "an animal does what it has to do." Isn't this what the human animal has to do?

Yes. Which is why we couldn't stick at being hunters. The basic design failure meant that our chief asset—conscious intelligence—would, at the service of aggression, curiosity, territoriality, xenophobia, dominance, and all the other raw material, simply run off on its own tracks. This we call imagination—*this* is what this animal does as opposed to others (some of which are intelligent enough).

So you are suggesting that the inability of intelligence to have its *own* values is the major design failure?

In a way. Some people have claimed values for intelligence—or its product science. For example, disinterestedness has been canvassed. But there is no evidence that it is intelligence (or reason or science) per se that is disinterested.

But surely it must suspend judgements for its operation. It cannot declare 2 + 2 "bad" and refuse to solve the equation. And surely this suspension, if brought often enough into play, would lead to a value being placed on disinterestedness?

Only in the pursuit of knowledge itself. And this knowledge, don't forget, by evolutionary fiat, is in the service of the brute raw material. It is only very recently that we have separated out certain people as pure specialists in the use of intelligence. And they are always divided in their notions of the ultimate use of their labors—usually on xenophobic grounds.

But again, if intelligence is a universal feature, cannot they claim that it should only be used for universal human good?

They can. Many have. But they are trapped. Who is to say that their evaluation is superior to that of someone who claims it should be used only for the good of the revolutionary proletariat? I told you religion was part of the problem.

You mean ideology?

O.K. Give it new and fancy names, but ultimately it is the response of the computer to the fact that it knows it exists and can articulate questions about this existence. In fact it finds it hard to operate at all without some answers to these questions, otherwise it lacks basic energy to go on computing.

Well, if it is so intelligent, why doesn't it come up with the answer?

Because there is no answer—at least not to the question as the computer feels obliged to pose it. Another design failure. But that doesn't stop it, in its ingenuity, from proposing numerous answers.

And what is so wrong with that?

Nothing intrinsically, except, for some reason, these answers seem to get hitched onto the raw material of xenophobia: we have our answer, and those with other answers are to be feared and eliminated if possible.

But what about religions of brotherly love?

They usually try to eliminate those who don't believe in religions of brotherly love. Those who believe in the triumph of the meek try to get rid of (or convert) those who believe in the triumph of the strong. And so on. The content of the ideology (if you must call it that) doesn't seem to matter. What matters is the belief in the idea—any idea.

Another design failure?

Yes. Once the computer was fully working it worked in terms of ideas (concepts, whatever). So when it began to question its own meaning it clearly assumed that the answer lay in some idea or set of ideas. Once given that it could not exist without the energy provided by an answer to its own answerless question, it clearly would become desperately attached to the ideas it had settled on. These were its engine, its motive power. Interference with them is the most damaging thing that faces the computer. Its alliance with the old xenophobic and aggressive raw material is thus fused. To threaten the idea is to threaten existence itself.

And the idea of science cannot transcend this?

Try threatening the idea of the idea of science (as variously interpreted) and see the response. Those revolutionaries who worshipped reason thought it quite reasonable to eliminate those who thought otherwise. It is the idea of the idea that rules, not the idea itself—not its content. Any idea—hence, for you, any ideology—is better than none.

Then if I understand the design failure, without attachment to ideas our intelligence cannot function, but once attached to ideas we are their prisoners and cannot function intelligently?

We can function intelligently in the sense that we can rationally adapt means to ends (try to kill the unbelievers with a knife as opposed to a lump of jello). But we cannot function dispassionately, disinterestedly, or reasonably, or even in our best long-run interests. If this is what you mean by intelligently, you are right.

I suppose I mean "intelligently" intelligently!

You probably mean what we used to call rationality—but in the special sense of having our ultimate self-preservation as a goal. If we see that short-term defense of our ideas is going to mean long-term destruction of them, then we should adjust.

Why don't we? Another design failure?

I'm afraid so. "Better dead than Red" sums it up? We lack effective long-term vision. For most people even a lifetime is too long to contemplate. In any case, it means contemplating death and we don't like that privilege the computer grants us. Also, we assume that it is the business of the computer to give us accurate information about the world. But this is doubtful. It is more likely that the thing gives us selective and optimistic information.

But surely this would have been an evolutionary disaster?

Not at all. The creature evolved to act, not to contemplate reality. The brain-computer gives us just enough information to make an adaptive action possible, then floods us with morphine to make us feel it will be possible, and adrenaline to help make it possible.

But freed from the need to act, surely it can behave rationally?

As I said before, only in a limited sphere—that of pure knowledge. Outside pure reason all is in the realm of practical reason—of action.

And in this world the rational, disinterested products of science have little place except, almost literally, as tools.

And these tools, this technology, are also handmaidens?

This would be more readily agreed to, I think. But what people forget is that 90 percent of so-called science is technology. And by a queer twist, the very value of disinterestedness that science and technology pretend to, renders them the even more perfect handmaidens of the xenophobic ideas.

But surely the idea that Mankind—that the whole species—should be saved, would solve the problem; everyone would adhere to it?

As people have pointed out, this might work if we were threatened by martians. Short of that it runs up against the formidable combination we have discussed: the alliance of the computer's dedication to the idea with the tendency to xenophobia, and the short-run vision and the inaccurate brain. People will find a way to differ about how the species should be saved and fight about that.

The xenophobia is part of the design failure? But why?

Same reason. It served a useful purpose when we were dispersed. It probably helped set the boundaries of breeding populations—language helped.

How could that be?

Has it ever occurred to you to ask why we speak so many different languages? We could all speak the same. But, given the capacity for language as such, we can develop infinite different ones. The paleolithic "linguistic tribe" was about 5,000 (our outer limits of tolerance?). The local group about 50 (our comfortable limit?).

Was the point of this to do with breeding, then?

Probably. You don't marry those you can't talk to. Of course, you can kill off their males and incorporate the women and the children—who would rapidly learn your language. This would have worked very well as an evolutionary mechanism, again, as long as we were dispersed. The species was not threatened.

Where did it go wrong?

Ideas are couched in language. Language groups that succeeded grew enormously at the expense of others. The xenophobia got out of hand. From being a boundary mechanism it became a vehicle for the propagation of ideas. People did not have even to share the same natural language to share the same ideas and to be attached to them with xenophobic ferocity. There had been no ideological differences between tribes; they fought over real issues. But soon whole bodies of people—even linguistically distinct—began fighting over ideas to which they were attached. The confluence of these mechanisms led to a backfiring of the system.

But the tribes surely hated the ideas of the other tribes—their customs and so on. This was part of the xenophobia, wasn't it?

Sometimes they hated them, sometimes feared them, sometimes despised them, sometimes respected them, sometimes admired them. But they didn't fight because of the ideas—not to protect or promulgate them. They fought over women or territory or whatever. It was the marriage of the attachment to the idea with the tribal xenophobia, carried beyond tribal boundaries, that led to disaster. Nations, religions, movements, cults, causes, parties—all artificial entities—came to behave like tribes with ideas as totems.

So what had been a useful evolutionary mechanism backfired?

Exactly.

How can that happen? Is it unique to us?

In a sense it happens every time a species fails to adapt to changing circumstances and becomes extinct—which is the evolutionary rule by the way, not the exception. Our case is however unique.

Because we know what is happening?

Because we not only know what is happening but because the capacity to know what is happening is also the cause of what is happening! Now that is unique—if you're after the real marks of human uniqueness!

So that is why reason, science, technology, and religion can't save us?

Yes. For what produces them is the same design failure that produces the problems they are supposed to solve—indeed they are part of the problem. They are products of the unholy marriage that is the design failure.

The logic of this is that any of our efforts to solve the problem are doomed to make it worse, is it not?

If the efforts remain within the vicious circle we have explored this must be so. Any redoubling of scientific or religious (ideological) effort is likely to exacerbate the problem. Those of us who have urged a species-centered ethic, for example, have been now classified as a cult with the marks of the devil, and all kinds of tribes with their idea-totems are ranged against us. To save the species-ethic, then, we may have to destroy a lot of the species. Scarcely the outcome we intended, but part of the logic of the system. Someone, as I said, will always differ about how the species should be saved, or which bit of it, or something such.

Because they have to?

Yes. An idea only has to be slightly different to become a point of attachment and a focus of suspicion and fanaticism.

You haven't mentioned fanaticism as such before. Another design failure?

Yes. It's an outgrowth of xenophobia. The xenophobic fanatic is a tribal chauvinist—the one who claims the world for his tribe. There were probably such: the Genghis Khans, the Alexanders. But they didn't do much long-run harm because—and we're back to this—they couldn't affect the survival of the species.

But now a few fanatics can?

Unfortunately that is the way. And they need not be foaming at the mouth fanatics. It is the degree of single-minded devotion to the idea that marks the fanatic. A seemingly cool decision that "democracy shall not perish without a fight" for example, could mean the end. This could also be a rational decision, given the premises, and one aided by all the computer information needed to augment the computer-brain. But it would be a fanatic decision, and hence a very human and very likely one. Of course, the foaming-mouth fanatics can be just as destructive—they are not usually as efficient.

And people connive in their own destruction?

Of course. The tribe is endangered—at any costs save the tribe. The idea is threatened—at any cost protect the idea. The result may be death, but without the idea we are dead anyway, so let it roll. I wonder how many realize just how inerradicably deep this is in the human mechanism? At once the reason for our staggering success and the built-in self-destruct device at the same time? Swift knew it was *the* danger—but of course he couldn't have known the evolutionary causes. But we will fight over which end of a boiled egg to crack.

People do oppose war.

Yes—and then define those who share that idea as their tribe and proceed to attack quite violently the opposition. Few people are as vicious to their opponents as the apostles of peace.

You are too cynical. What about the nonviolents?

Don't you see, we can't escape? This is another form of fanaticism (sometimes you have to be violent to do good) and it is the fanaticism that is the enemy. Every form of fanaticism (or ideology again, if you like) claims moral superiority—but what we need is an absence of fanaticism, not just another version, however pacific.

And this we cannot have?

No, because (remember the argument) the attachment to the idea is so basic a necessity (however simple or mundane the idea) that we need it to function at all. Hence we can only be fanatical in our dislike of fanatics. The Cretan liar always wins.

I'm sure that all this simply means that people have to have ideas or opinions in order to be able to act at all.

It does, but from the simple expansion of this rule comes all the paradox of our human existence. Animals don't have opinions, and they act.

They also become extinct.

But they don't know that this can happen. We do know and we let it happen anyway.

If you are right, our very knowing is what in our case causes it to happen. (I think.) But couldn't it have happened without our knowing being the cause?

Yes, of course—as with all other nonself-conscious species, including those closely related to us that are no more. But our absurd paradox is this: we should be able to avert the disaster that inevitably awaits a species since we know it can happen and can, theoretically, take steps to see that it doesn't.

But we won't?

No.

You seem confident of this. Why?

Because of my attachment to an idea.

What?

That Nature cannot be cheated. The law of extinction cannot be avoided by knowing of its existence. So Nature builds in an ingenious device: any species that comes to know of the nature of its own existence will use that knowledge to ensure its own extinction. It's quite beautiful really.

So there is no breaking out of the vicious circle? We are trapped in its premises?

I cherish a forlorn hope that some incredible change of cosmic gears might happen—some evolutionary change so profound (a quadrupling of the lifespan perhaps?) that it would change all the rules. But should it happen we might be forced to admit that what then existed was a successor species and not Homo sapiens at all—so the paradox would remain. We would not have become extinct, but our genes would be so changed we would be a different species. And this might more readily happen in the wake of nuclear wars with massive radiation and an astronomically increased mutation rate. From this a new species might emerge that would solve the paradox. This one never will.

I don't believe what you say, but I would fight to the death for your right to say it, of course.

Of course.

COMING OF AGE IN JUST ABOUT EVERYWHERE*

This is a word of consolation
For those who fear the confrontation
Between the social and genetic

Before you all become frenetic
Let's try to figure what it means
This war of culture and the genes
The torment that provokes the colic
Twixt chromosomal and symbolic

It does not take a smart detective
To see it's all in the perspective
Pursue the symbols if you must
You then can take the genes on trust
But don't dismiss as blind or comic
Pursuit of matters teleonomic
Avoid the tediousness of faction
Through gene and culture interaction
As scientists you can wax lyrical—
The question has become empirical!

Culture aint worth a heap of beans
If it can't propogate the genes
But if not fortified by culture
The genes are doomed to quick sepulture†
So let this question lift the gloom

*Except, if Woody Allen is right, certain parts of New Jersey
†Acknowledgement to R. Browning, "The Grammarian's Funeral"

"Who gives what or which to whom?"
And if you're really very keen
Try empathizing with the gene

The Gene is not on pleasure bent
On replication it's intent
Though sex results from its demand
The kicks are only second hand
Its puritanical devotion
To putting further Genes in motion
While organisms have the fun
Is worthy   when all's said and done
Compare the endless aggravation
Of Culture's aimless dissipation
The way symbolic systems fatten
On each unwholesome culture pattern
And try with frivolous invention
To twist the sombre Gene's intention

The Selfish Gene brooks no excuse
The inner voice screams "reproduce"
(The consequence is less complex
We hear it as "indulge in sex")
However much we symbolize
The Gene is ultimately wise
In every culture upon earth
We screw a lot   and then give birth
The Gene will never know   you see
The point of the diversity
It's ends that interest the Genes
So their concern is not with means
Choose any way you like to mate
One thing is sure—they replicate
Since replication is the game
All diverse cultures are the same
In the long run genetic view
(Except perhaps the very few
Which fail to replicate at all
But they gone beyond recall)

Of interest though we're not bereft
The only question that is left
Is fascinating   you'll allow
"So mate   so replicate   but HOW?"
It does not matter in the end
But still we can observe the trend
For in the long run   as Keynes said
We lose our interest   being dead

So cheer up social scientist
Variety's a finite list
But there to keep you occupied
(Occasionally boggle-eyed)
As ponderously you pursue
Each turn of the symbolic screw
And watch the figures weave and prance
Their patterns in the cultural dance
That goes unheeded and unseen
By the indifferent   patient Gene

MUSIC OF THE SPHERES

Who choreographs the dance of life
God   or Balanchine?
No   Mendel and his wrinkled peas—
or something in between

Who orchestrates the song of youth
God   or Borodin?
No   Jacob Monod Watson Crick—
a regulator gene

What promulgates the will to live
God   (that passer by?)
No   Mindless protein molecules
that don't know how to die

THREE INTERRUPTIONS OF RATIONAL ARGUMENTS

(These were all "interludes," intended to comment on, while breaking up, the otherwise heavy-going arguments of the three papers mentioned in the introduction to this book. The first was to have been in an article, "The Violent Imagination." The second is from the as-yet-unpublished "Consciousness out of Context," to be published in a future book called The Search for Society. *This contains a critical look at Daniel Bell's* The Coming of Post-Industrial Society, *hence the epigraph. It may look like free verse but it isn't. It is intended to sound like a literal translation of chorus from a Greek tragedy, hence "first stasimon." The last one is from "Inhuman Nature and Natural Rights." See introduction again.)*

. . . .

THE WALL
(Christmas Eve: Jerusalem)

You scare me
        Wall
                To take me by surprise
out of the dark like that was wrong
                        You draw
me on   you loom   you threaten
                      Still   I wear

177

an alien cap so I might touch you
                              Wall
might join the pious ants who scuffle round
your ponderous stone feet   so I might mix
my fingers with their fingers while they probe
your cavities obscenely with their scraps
of futile paper   sad   mundane requests
"Please God   take care of Rachel"
                                        Put it back

I should have gone to Bethlehem but
                              Wall
I came to you instead
                        I don't know why
Perhaps because I don't believe that myth
they seared my childhood with   but you are real
stone idol
          golden Wall

                        You are alive
You are electric   and you seem to sing
You speak not just to Jews   I hear you
                              Wall
in some mad inner ear
                        She said to me
"I saw men die so I could be here"
                              Wall
She said that as she went to stroke your stones
said it with faith in some Judaic god
that moves me not at all
                        She came away
in tears
          I did not weep   But listen
                              Wall
accept my infidelic touch   I could
not bear rejection
                    Let me hide in you
Your gold and throbbing stones cry out like flesh
to be embraced
                and yet your touch is cold

I fear you
        Wall
                for men will die again
not for their god   but you
                        And I know this
I have no reverence for that Hebrew god
that gloomy   vengeful chauvinist
                        and yet
I know that I could worship you
                        old Wall
and for your stones we all perhaps might die

PATRIMONY FOR A POSSIBLE POSTERITY
(first stasimon)

> *". . . the duplex nature of man himself—the mur-*
> *derous aggression, from primal impulse, to tear*
> *apart and destroy."*
>
> Daniel Bell, *The Coming of*
> *Post-Industrial Society*

What shall we tell them?
What shall we tell the survivors?

What shall we leave them
Those who may remain?

Why should they listen?
Why should they pay attention?
We talked ourselves into annihilation
We argued our way into death
We destroyed ourselves with words
How can they learn from our experience
When our experience led to their near extinction?

We can tell them what to avoid.
That is all that is left to tell the survivors.
If there are any survivors.
We can tell them what we did wrong
If we can recognize what we did wrong
If we dare admit our mistakes
And admit them now.

But how can we admit to what we
    do not understand?
How can we tell the survivors what not
    to repeat?
Will it be obvious to them?

Will they say, "They did it badly,
    but we can start again
We can do it right this time."
And will they get it right?
Will it be so obvious what went wrong?
Hindsight has not helped us so far
Will it help the survivors?

What shall we tell them to avoid?
We cannot tell them what to construct
We do not know what to construct
Every effort at construction is a failure.
At destruction we are geniuses
We were always best at destruction
Since the first butchering
The first attack on the herds
Since the first deserts and wastelands
We have destroyed like true artists.

We can tell them to avoid destruction.
But how to tell them why they
    cannot avoid it?
How to tell them why their pleasure
    is most sweet and delicate when they destroy
Tell them to avoid ecstacy?
Tell them to avoid the delusion
    of power destruction offers?
They know the power of destruction
They will have seen the end of their
    civilization
They will have seen their cities gone
    to dust and their lakes to filth
    and their oceans to emptiness
All this they will have seen.
They will not need to be told to
    avoid destruction
They will need to be told why they
    need to destroy
Or why they cannot despite the best

intentions avoid their joy
in destruction.
They will need to be told to forgo
their joy.

Is this a thing to tell the survivors?
Those few who have lived through
the destruction?
To avoid destruction you must
destroy part of yourselves?

Is that our legacy to
the survivors—
Torn, desperate and wretched—
A paradox?

REASON IS, AND OUGHT TO BE, FUTILE

The function of intelligence it seems
(reflecting on the fine futility
of thinking about loving you instead
of simply doing it) is to infiltrate
confusion among the emotions—cramping and
controling   confining and inhibiting
what otherwise might be direct   proud   fierce
untroubled by concern with consequence
and prejudicial to good order and
discipline among the regimented passions.

Can I not love you and not count the costs—
forsee   foretell   predict   prognosticate—
balance the mindless consumated swift
magnetic nonsense on the one hand with
the other sentient sensible handful of
consideration consequence and cause?

Love is a feeling not an argument
It has an end but so far no solution—
a goal—but no deductive reasoning
can reach that goal or realize that end

Reason is not   dear David   as you said
slave of the passions   nor ought it to be
(and you derived an ought from something quite
so fragile—so sensational—an is?)
Reason is God's gift to man because
it makes him doubt the brutish   nasty   short
and natural   in him   and so makes him man

But that leaves me a questioner when
I want to be a lover   and the two
are seemingly at war in me   and this
is how it should be else we are not men
and would just copulate and never write
these tortured verses as a compliment
to cunning intellect that makes us men
and yet unmans us in the making   Help!

LYRICS ON THE FEMALE ENIGMA
(again)

. . . .

THREE POSSIBILITIES

There are those women who inspire lust
for some small reason like the way a dress
clings to a limb   the mouth pulsates   the eye
droops slightly   It inflames but does not last

Some others radiate a childish need—
a vulnerable blink   a nervous touch
a tender imploration   These can draw
but not inflame   not drive the cool brain mad

Very rarely there are those whose hurt
and restless hardness makes its own demand
that's neither love nor lust   but need to tame
the spirit's panther   yet not break its heart

GIRLS WHO LOST THEIR FATHERS

Girls who lost their fathers   who are doomed
to drift through life like souls condemned   will stray
forever in a limbo of their own
Sealed in the past their spirits lie entombed

Their bodies meanwhile try to find a way
to hide the truth   they must survive alone

Some lacking trust in trust their bodies turn
to many lovers   intimate with none
Some desperately cling to older men
for restoration   and they rarely learn
that they are self-deceived   once it is gone
the father's love cannot return again

The lovers' contract always has fine print
The father's love seemed unconditional
Age does not guarantee a thing   but then
I do not even have the heart to hint
that all is futile   nothing will annul
the grief   however fatherlike their men

But though they lost their fathers they are not
as stricken as girls never loved at all
At least the fantasy can act like dope
and phantom fathers in a ghostly plot
endowed with other bodies can recall
a sad incestuous memory of hope

PROSPECT OF NUCLEAR WINTER

After the desolation and the death
uprose the sun-obscuring dust   and then
the creeping cold that turned the world to ice
a smooth round shining ball   except without
the sun it could not shine   But when the dust
had cleared a little   there the beauty hung
flashing and gleaming through the shredded veil
(a youthful widow contemplating sex)

and in a galaxy far far away
an eye protruding from a stalk projecting
from a gigantic brain was pressed against
the eyepiece of a super telescope
And for a moment this superior
intelligence observed the flashing orb
and thought   in fractions of a nanosecond
that it would call it − < #+ ¯ %ˆ &   *¯{:+−!¯
"crystal(ine) planet-the"   then turned away
to its far more important work   the planning
of the ultimate war made necessary
by the discovery of a logical
contradiction in the arguments
between galactic ideologies
And in a parallel universe   a far
far far superior intelligence
noticed this blip in time   and since for it
time was running backwards (at the time)
it saw the end result and named it thus
(I translate roughly   for they spoke in math)
"consciousness = crystal universe"

BULLFIGHT AT ALTAMIRA:
THE SEA AT SANTA MARTA

(Colombia, 1981)

La vaca del viejo mundo
pasaba su triste lengua
sobre un hocico de sangres
derramadas en la arena,
y los toros de Guisando,
casi muerte y casi piedra,
mugieron como dos siglos
hartos de pisar la tierra.

Federico García Lorca, *Llanto por la muerta de*
Ignacio Sánchez Mejías

I do not find
The Hanged Man. Fear death by water.
I see crowds of people, walking round in a ring.

T. S. Eliot, *The Waste Land*

. . . .

ALTAMIRA DE COELLO, TOLIMA, AUG. 8

Conquistadores brought the name that tells
it all   if you can break the code   It was
Altamira   They added (Portuguese)
de Coello   but all was in the name
The paleolithic brain that painted bulls
is the same brain that manufactures rockets

187

to send brains to the moon to play at golf
But here we're free of such banality
inheriting direct through Mithras and
the cult of Minotaurus to the roots
of Indo-European mysteries
And here at Altamira de Coello
we free ourselves from all the tinselled pomp
that troubled Spaniards weave around the bull
to pacify their Catholic guilt when in
their pagan hearts they feel participation
in things that mock their Christian piety

Because we know we die   that all things die
so we can make a cult of death   (or love
or food or self-denial or compassion)
We are nature's cultists but the cult
of death defines us most—not ritual
The animals perfected ritual
before the first australopithecine
had ever chipped a stone—we ritualize
as easily as we digest   But cults
are products of our pure imagination
and gorge upon the ritual tendency
to feed the cultic appetite
                              The bull
does what it has to do to be a bull
At Altamira in old Spain a man
painted a bull   So simple   Yet consider
he did not have to   Nor do we today
at Altamira de Coello have
to dance the dangerous dance   And yet we must
We do not have to   yet we have no choice
We need not make a cult of death   but how
to face the fact of death without a cult?
So we transfer it to a cult of life
and Mithras and the bleeding bull become
(through Persian soma like our own?) a death
changed into life
                    The cycle turns
The bull must fertilize   the god must die

the bull-calf lives   the god must rise again
to fertilize and die eternally

Old Altamirans killed both bull and horse
and did not live with them or dance with them
But they did paint them   and the first remove
from ritual to cult was realized
That painter was the universal man
Both bull and horse were tamed   and in the herds
of some Caucasian mob was born a race
that lived upon the anvil of the earth
forged from the fury of the fire of heaven
the rivers   plains   the horse   the sky   the bull
the restless movement and the endless wars
til it became a fierce particular
of that old Altamiran universal
And even when the matriarchal plot
had rendered them as fat and slow as oxen
and made them cautious tillers of the earth
there still were those—those brains of Altamira—
who never did   who never could forget
the bull that was their life   As more than meat
but as the thing sent down in fire and thunder
to test their manhood and to make them men
(For men must make their men   There is no way
that nature makes a human male a man
A rigid penis is no use unless
its owner's arms can turn aside a bull
or paint it on the walls of Altamira)

Here we are at the heart   at Altamira
the place where when the bull and he together
perform their ritual   the matador
stands in the sun and sand alone   apalled
at being (without knowing) at the source
of all that makes him his particular kind
of human creature   and that makes him man
Here there are the bulls   the sky   and us
We do not fight   we dance   and in the dance
so little intervenes   (a curious crowd

of visitors   paisanos   Some are high
on soma—sister of the bull itself—
and some   the friends of Dionysus are
a little sacred with aguardiente)
Stark in the dust there is the rough wood ring
the sun   the sky   the bulls   and in the ring
waits symbol-sodden man   drunk only with
the mystery of loving perfect death

And so despite the mother goddess they
continued with the ballet of the bull
and with the passage of the years forgot
except in some intuitive recess
of racial and of species memory
the meaning of the dancer and the dance

But here at Altamira we remember
because there is so little to distract
And I   novitiate   careless with the cape
invite the charge with casual invasion
of that enchanted circle which the bull
has claimed as his   And when he turns and when
with lowered horns starts on his sudden charge
and I too numb for fear yet drunk with truth
turn him aside—a hundred thousand years
of history are frozen in the heat
and swirl about me in the sand   and enter
my nostrils from the mingling of our sweat

And when I turn too slowly and our bodies
crash in a mad embrace of man and beast
my brain explodes with mysteries too intense
for verse or science or philosophy
I only know the bull and I must die
and that together we can make it perfect
and in that making   in that calm perfection
something is fulfilled that at its root
is what makes me a man and him a bull
and is as necessary to our beings as
the blood that we each spill   that we both share

SIERRA NEVADA DE SANTA MARTA, RIO DON DIEGO, AUG. 20

The waves at Santa Marta charge at me
and throw me to the sand   and when I try
to gain the shore they suck me back again
I can't believe it is impersonal
so fierce and so particular the fury
the sea affronts me with   I am afraid
of death by drowning   Nothing has endowed
the waves with instinct   Death   you say   is death
But I will take death from the bull   and he
will take it from me also   With respect
Because we share so much   Not so the sea
that alien idiot ferocity
Canute   old Dane   there with your cape of words
you taught a lesson deeper than you knew
One cannot turn aside the charge of waves
A death from drowning has no meaning   and
one cannot make it meaningful   it is
"an accident"   a misery of chance
The bull death is a mystery of choice
a bullfight a memento mori   so
I choose   therefore I am   therefore I choose
the beauty of the bulls of Altamira
and shun the mindless danger of the sea

Protestant   alone and without God
the universe is only what I make it—
this curious cosmic accident   and yet
I'm caught in the inevitable flow
of nature   and if then I must impose
a meaning on the accident I claim
a death of my own choosing   (since my birth
was yet another accidental quirk)
As I was born through semen   blood   and pain
so let me die the bull death and complete
the circle   and with one symbolic stroke

191

impose my meaning on the natural
and yet cheat nature by cooperation
because what I impose is nature's will—
we struggled he and I   and he survived

How human thus to die by paradox
and in that death assert humanity
flinging a cape at accident and mocking
the imbecile indifference of chance

PSALM ONE HUNDRED AND FIFTY-ONE

nulla fugae ratio, nulla spes: omnia muta
omnia sunt deserta, ostentant omnia letum

Catullus

How is it possible to expect that Mankind will take
Advice, when they will not so much as take warning.

Swift

. . . .

Thou holdest in thine hand, O child of man,
    the power to destroy thyself: and who shall
    save thee? Who shall stay thine hand?
Shalt thou save thyself: Look into thine own
    heart; multiply thy vision a billion times
    four;
Does it shout salvation? O miserable echo:
    it whispers—help!

Shall thy great leaders save thee, child of heroes?
Shall Gandhi, Churchill, Stalin, King?
Shall Begin, Khomeini, Roosevelt, Ho?
Shall Kennedy, Sadat, Qaddafi, Jesus?
Shall Moses, Akhenaton, Joan of Arc?
The fanatics of strength: the megalomaniacs of
    Peace?

With the fateful formula: xenophobia plus
    fanaticism plus the instinct of the

herd equals power—for me, my children,
my likenesses, my ideas.

Shall ideas save thee, child of mind?
Shall empiricism, idealism, nominalism, racism?
Shall romanticism, pacifism, feminism, positivism?
Shall predestination, reincarnation, transubstantiation,
    verification?
Utilitarianism, pragmatism, relativism, pantheism,
Anarchism, humanism, creationism, scientism,
Behaviorism, stoicism, nationalism, solipsism,
Evolutionism, rationalism, structuralism,
    Marxism, progress or original sin?

Shall thy philosophers save thee, child of
    knowledge?
Shall thy men of science man the breach
    and save thee, child of the experimentum crucis?
Shall thy physicians heal thy sickness, child
    of flesh?
Shall the knowledge of thy teachers save thee,
    child of learning?
Shall the conscience of the rulers of earth?
Shall the meekness of earth's inheritors?

Shall religions save thee, child of faith?
Shall Catholicism, shall the Polish Pope,
The Anglican, Unitarian, Baptist, Presbyterian,
Lutheran, Orthodox, Methodist, Congregationalist,
The Maronite, Copt or the Countess of Huntingdon's
    Connection?
Shall the Buddhists, the Hindus, the
    Confucians or Taoists,
The Swedenborgians, Christian Scientists, Mormons
    or Shakers,
The Church of God in Christ, the Church of Christ
    in God,
The Bahaists, the Sunni, the Sufi, the Judaic,
The Shiite, the Holy Rollers or the Peculiar
    People?

Shall Shinto, or Zoroastrians or the Old
    Believers?

Shall religion save thee or divide thee
    O thou quivering, devoted faithful?
Turn to it for Truth; it gives thee truth;
    so choose thy Truth and die for it; thou
    splendid martyr!

Shall patriotism save thee?
My country right or wrong:
The jingoistic, xenophobic high?
Pursuit of our manifest destiny?
Recapturing our sacred national territory;
Regaining our sacred national freedom;
Exploiting our sacred national wealth;
Protecting our sacred national borders;
Restoring our sacred national virtue;
Destroying our sacred national enemies;
Defending our unimpeachable national honor,
Revenging the insult to our beloved national flag;
Reviving our virtually unspoken national language;
And above all having our uneconomic national
    airline.
To spend more than we earn; borrow more
    then we can repay;
To equip our national troops for all the
    above purposes with weapons we cannot
    afford;
To raise the standard of living of our people from
    terrible to tolerable with luck;
To be a light to lighten other nations with
    our proud example.

And the little nationalisms—shall they save
    thee, child of the tribe?
The heartland of the xenophobia, fanaticism
    and instinct of the herd?
Shall Basque, Catalan, Provençal, Breton,
    Corsican?

Shall Ukrainian, Georgian, Serbian, Croatian,
    Montenegrin?
Shall Palestinian, Kurdish, Baluchi, Québecois,
    Biafran?
Shall Welsh, Zionist, Bugandan, Punjabi,
    Assamese?
For as thou prophesiest their decline, so
    shall they rise, feeding the tumor
    of xenophobia, fanaticism and the
    instinct of the herd.
And fearing thine own superstates thou
    sayest:
"Yea, this is good: the people are returning
    to their sense of identity; of place: this
    is more human."
And indeed it is, child of the tumor that feeds our
    humanity;
And even as thou sayest, another child dies
    shouting slogans for the tribal crusade.
For will the tribes in their folk wisdom
    fail to perfect the weapon which is
    their god?
And will they shrink from using it if the
    tribal honor is affronted, its lands
    possessed by strangers?
Yes—give them back their spears!
At least in savagery we are safe from
    ultimate destruction, child of the weapon.
But remember, child of the pogrom and the
    massacre, to carry thine own spear,
    and lock thy door at twilight, and put
    thy trust in no one.
And remember the knowledge of the weapon
    that will end forever the enemies of
    the tribe;
Remember the knowledge, child of progress,
    that thou canst not take away;
And remember that knowledge is the tumor's
    slave.

Where shalt thou turn?
Shall technology save thee, child of ingenuity?
Shall science save thee, child of intellect?
Shall computers, electronics, optics, polymers;
Plasma physics, micro-chip information storage
And retrieval; nuclear fission and fusion?
Shall gene-splicing, solar water pumps;
Robots, artificial intelligence, space shuttles?
Shall green revolutions, herbicides, pesticides;
Defoliants, synthetic fertilizers, dams?
Shall cybernetics, systems theory, multiphase
Analysis, multidimensional scaling, feedback?
Shall linear programming, Markov chains,
Stochastic processes, topology, field theory,
Quantum mechanics, quarks, quasars or
    red dwarfs?

Where shalt thou look now God hath deserted thee?
Thou hast nothing but these mirrors of thyself:
Art thou safe from thyself, child of fantasy?
In the hollows of thine heart hast thou not
    destroyed us all a thousand times in
    thine omnipotence?
And are those who hold the power to destroy—
    children re-born to real omnipotence—
    more than thou art, bastard child of Cain?
Look upon them, see thyself, and weep.

You demand guidance, you ask for advice; be not cynical
    be constructive you cry.
You ask for advice, children of necessity; I say
Remember the Manicheans, they gave you advice; I say
Remember the Shakers, they gave you advice; I say
Remember the Albigenses; I say remember all the sages
Who thundered "Abandon Sex!" "Abandon Procreation!"
That was advice. Why did you not take it? I am the
Shaker/Manichean/Albigensian of ideas. I cry unto thee
"Abandon Nationalism" I exhort thee   "Abandon religious zeal"
I plead "Abandon hatred of the stranger, your giant bureaucracies,

Your greed for power, your lust for progress"   And I cry
With the same result as they.   Did you abandon sex?   If I cry
Will you listen?   Will you abandon this eroticism of the soul?
Do not ask for advice you know you cannot heed.

Thou hast built incredible engines of travel
    and manufacture; of pleasure and of
    science.
Thou hast extended thy memory with machines
    and improved the speed of thought with them.
Thou hast probed the nature of matter with
    thy machines down to the machinery
    of life itself.
But nowhere hast thou probed thyself, child
    of invention.
Nowhere hast thou probed the tumor that
    lives on thee and by which thou
    art forced to live.
Nowhere hast thou discovered why thy
    genius for machines leadeth
    inevitably to engines of ultimate
    destruction.

Thy most perfect thinking machines cannot
    answer thy most simple, most desperate
    question: what shall we do to be
    saved?

Where shalt thou search?

Shall thine assemblies save thee, child of
    rhetoric?
Shall parliaments, dumas, dáils, assemblés
    nationales?
Shall senates, congresses, cabinets, caucuses;
Disarmament conferences, arms limitation talks;
Leagues of cities, leagues or unions of states
    or nations;
Comminterms, central committees, United Workers
    of the World in conclave?

Shall thy parties save thee, child of faction?
Shall conservatives, liberals, socialists;
Radicals, centrists, slightly left of center?
Shall radical social Christian democrats;
Christian democratic radical socialists?
Bolsheviks, mensheviks, narodniki;
Popular fronts, national fronts, coalitions;
Progressives, reactionaries, single issue parties;
Mugwumps, know nothings, monarchists
    or whigs?

Shall thy teachers save thee, child of learning?
Shall colleges, lycées, universities, foundations;
Polytechnics, gymnasia, institutes of
Advanced study for the solution of everything;
Career development grants and genius awards?
Shall faculties of arts, science and humanities?
Shall presidents, vice-chancellors and deans; shall professors
Emeritus, regius, distinguished, adjunct
    and part-time?

Shall causes save thee, passionate child of
    faction?
Shall anti-war, shall anti-waste, shall
    anti-pollution?
Shall C.N.D., shall S.D.P., shall Solidarność;
    The Hitler Youth, Young England, the Young Turks;
Children's crusades, the Green Party;
Zionist Leagues of Youth, Young Communists?
Shall Boy Scouts, Weathermen, Gay Liberation;
The P.L.O., the Ku Klux Klan, The League of Women
Voters, the Young Republicans, the Red Brigade;
The A.C.L.U., the National Front, Save the Whales;
The Moral Majority, the Provisional or
    Official I.R.A.?

Shall capitalism save thee, child of affluence?
Ever afraid of boom and slump and the
    skeletal rattle in the trade cycle
    cupboard of stagflation, unemployment,

currency collapse, bank failure;
The cartels, trusts, multinationals, monopolies,
    oligopolies and O.P.E.C.;
Protectionism, laissez-faire, tariff controls
    and agreements?
Shall Texaco and U.S. Steel, B.P., United
    Fruit, Royal Dutch Shell;
General Motors, I.B.M., I.T. and T.(that was);
U.A.W.U., the Central Banks, the I.M.F.,
The E.E.C., the I.L.O., the World Bank, I.A.T.T.?

Shall the celebrities save thee, child of the
    stars?
In their narcissistic whirl around the galaxy
    of mega-admiration, the adulation of
    the herd?
Do the old gods go down giving way to:
    Grammies, Oscars, Emmies, Platinum discs;
    Gold medals, Nobels, Pulitzers, National
    Book Awards, literary luncheons, O.B.E.s
    Prix de this-and-that?
And when they join the causes and the parties
    and the religions, child of factiousness,
    dost thou feel safer when they twinkle there?

Shall the strong save thee, child of weakness?
Shall the will of the proletariat embedded
    in the party and its leaders give thee
    comfort with the promise of the withering
    away of the state when there shall be no
    purges, gulags, martial law, interrogations?
Shall the will of the people embedded
    in its always benign protectors, lull
    thee to security unless as an enemy
    of the State thy disappearance is
    deemed necessary for the public good
    until the next coup and the
    next round of disappearances?
Put thy trust in strength and thou shalt
    feel that strength undoubtedly, child
    of fear.

Shall thine institutions save thee, child
   of liberty?
Shall the separation of powers, one man one
   vote?
Shall due process, habeas corpus, judicial revue?
Shall cabinet responsibility, the single
   transferable vote?
Shall they? So thou hast believed, child of
   optimism.

There is nothing we can point to as worth saving
That has not sometime been an instrument
   of crude destructiveness.
To try to save it is at best a gamble.
Dost thou not see, child of paradox,
These lists of the agents of thine own destruction
Are the glorious creations of thine intellect?
(Add art and music, but these serve any masters.)
These powerful products of thine imagination
Are all that raiseth thee up to bring thee down.
The beast does what it must; we do what
   we imagine.
What price the outcome, child of the
   imagination; name the price?
The imagination runs riot like
   vegetation in a jungle.
We are nature's most incompetent
   gardeners.

As children we labored lovingly to build
A castle in the sand—a fairy palace
Of intricate and fragile beauty, knowing
That we built it to anticipate the
Wide-eyed awe, the thrill, the terror and
The pleasure, the sadness and the ecstasy
Of seeing its quick obliteration by the waves.
Adults learn to lie and say—"The waves
Will never come. We have a formula
(Consult the lists) to hold them back."
But children know—and that is why
They build. The children lie not neither

Do they spin webs of ideas to hide their
Gleeful sorrow at ultimate destruction.

But thou, bright educated child of hope
    still criest, "Yes, yes this one shall save
    us, this is the truth/he is the truth/they
    are the truth."
Shalt thou protest, child of indignation,
    "But yes, these are good/she is good/
    this movement is good"?
Shalt thou insist, O child of righteousness,
    "But yes, let them listen unto us/him/
    her/them; let them hearken unto *us*,
    unto *our* words, and they shall be saved"?
And when the other answereth, child of
    conviction:
    "Nay, for it is *our* truth/his truth/
    the truth; so hearken unto *us* and
    learn the real truth," what wilt
    thou say, O child of contradiction?
And if I say unto thee, "There is no truth
    but there is every truth and the
    truth of truths is the war of all
    truths against all, and in this
    war there is no victory for truth
    but only the destruction of all truths"?
What wilt thou answer—or hast thou already
    begun to hate the question?
"I still have my truth, plague me not old
    man with thy cynicism; drink thy
    wine and be silent;
"For my truth shall triumph, shall redeem
    the world, shall stay the destructive hand."

O Blessed Child! How beautiful it would be
    to believe thy truth if only for the opium
    of hope.
But I have believed too many and the wine
    of conviction is vinegar in my mouth.
Once I would have said: "Better the flame

of thy useless passion than the timid
   turning to the self."
But now I know not such consolation.
The tumor that we feed on and that feeds us,
The xenophobia, zealotry and gullibility
   of man
Runs rampant through our billions.

No, child, it is not so easy now.

Once, in those days when it was very
   joy to be alive and young, the choice
   was easy: pick a cause, a simple
   truth—life, liberty or country,
   justice, freedom, love—and live
   and die for it. And if thou diest,
   if thousands died or hundreds of
   their thousands, no final harm was
   done, and always hope, hope, hope
   for better things to come made
   even life worth giving up.

To die now is to contribute to nothing.

The interglacial cometh to its end.
The ice looms waiting for its turn;
And that is our best hope, child of the ice.
If any of us stay to face the ice, perhaps
   we'll face it well; we'll be ourselves again.
If any should remain after the cold-eyed
   children of the survivors of the first
   ice have sent their terminal spearheads
   singing the final death song into the
   camps of their enemies;
If any should survive, the ice may cleanse;
The tumor may freeze into inactivity;
The children of the ice will walk the earth
   like gods . . .

As it was in the beginning

Glory be to the power of the idea;
Glory be to the hatred of the stranger;
Glory be to the lust for domination;
Glory be to the conviction of the leaders;
Glory be to the gullibility of the mob;
Glory be to the tumor that feeds us and
    on which we feed for it has left us
    in its greed for self-annihilation
    with the cruelest legacy of all;
It has robbed us of the chance to cheat
    our unbearable knowledge that we
    must die by dying to some purpose,
    and in that moment of death
    saying, "I died for better things to come."

Child, when nothing is to come, we have
    left thee nothing worthy
    of thy death.

Amen.